外交外事文书写作

主　编◎张　庆
副主编◎龙　凌/张　颖

四川外国语大学复合型国际化人才培养系列特色教材

总主编：刘玉梅/张　庆

时事出版社
北京

图书在版编目（CIP）数据

外交外事文书写作/张庆主编．—北京：时事出版社，2019.8

ISBN 978-7-5195-0320-8

Ⅰ.①外…　Ⅱ.①张…　Ⅲ.①外交事务—公文—写作　Ⅳ.①D802.5②C931.46

中国版本图书馆 CIP 数据核字（2019）第 081761 号

出版发行：时事出版社
地　　址：北京市海淀区万寿寺甲 2 号
邮　　编：100081
发行热线：（010）88547590　88547591
读者服务部：（010）88547595
传　　真：（010）88547592
电子邮箱：shishichubanshe@sina.com
网　　址：www.shishishe.com
印　　刷：北京旺都印务有限公司

开本：787×1092　1/16　印张：14.75　字数：240 千字
2019 年 8 月第 1 版　2019 年 8 月第 1 次印刷
定价：88.00 元

主　编：张　庆

副主编：龙　凌　张　颖

编委会　（以姓氏笔画为序）：

马　彦　王贤林　甘　勇　龙　凌　朱天祥
朱菊芹　刘　芳　邱晓芳　张　庆　张　颖
陈　宏　周　文　周思邑　贾思梅　崔亦歌
梁　立　梁诗闻　谌华侨

总序

Foreword

当今世界正处在大发展、大变革、大调整时期。世界多极化、经济全球化深入发展，科技进步日新月异，人才竞争日趋激烈。我国正处在改革发展的关键阶段，经济建设、政治建设、文化建设、社会建设以及生态文明建设全面推进，工业化、信息化、城镇化、市场化、国际化深入发展，人口、资源、环境压力日益加大，经济发展方式加快转变，这一切都凸显了提高国民素质，培养创新人才的重要性和紧迫性。《国家中长期教育改革和发展规划纲要（2010—2020年）》明确提出人才培养要加强国际交流与合作。“坚持以开放促改革、促发展。开展多层次、宽领域的教育交流与合作，提高我国教育国际化水平。借鉴国际上先进的教育理念和教育经验，促进我国教育改革发展，提升我国教育的国际地位、影响力和竞争力。适应国家经济社会对外开放的要求，培养大批具有国际视野、通晓国际规则、能够参与国际事务和国际竞争的国际化人才。”

培养复合型国际化人才已然成为我国众多高等院校的人才培养目标。复合型人才培养强调人才的基本知识、技能和素质的培养，讲究知识结构的多元化与合理组合，而国际化人才培养更加侧重国际化理念和意识的建立，以及在全球环境中实际操作的能力。根据国家人事部的统计，目前我国高层次人才占人才资源总量的5.5%，而高级人才中的国际化人才则更少，足见国际化人才的珍贵与稀缺。在我国企业不断迈向国际化经营的进程中，国际化人才的问题如不解决，必将成为制约我国企业进一步发展的资源瓶颈。

四川外国语大学以党的十九大精神为指导，全面贯彻党的教育方针，主动对接“一带一路”和“中国文化走出去”等国家重大战略需求以及重庆市内陆开放高地建设需求，对内实施供给侧结构性改革、创新人才培养模式，对外强化合作办学、走产学研合作之路，培养国家和地方用得上、受欢迎的高级外语和涉外人才，以“双一流”为引领，把学校建设成高水平的应用研究型外国语大学。在人才培养模式上，学校及时瞄准社会对实用型外语人才的大量需求，不断进行教育教学改革，突出创新精神和实用能力的培养，注重跨专业知识和技能的扩充以及综合素养的提高，发展学科专业优势，增强人才培养特色。为此，我们编写了“四川外国语大学复合型国际化人才培养系列特色教材”，包括《外交外事文书写作》《联合国研究》《领事保护实验教学案例分析》《时政视听说》等。我们希望该系列特色教材能进一步推动学校人才培养的国际化进程，进而为重庆打造内陆开放高地提供政策建议和智力支持。

参与本系列特色教材编撰的作者大都来自四川外国语大学国际关系学院。学院坚持“双轮驱动、复合发展”理念，以“国际事务导向、语言能力并重”为宗旨，积极探索“英语＋涉外事务”和“外交/国政＋英语”人才培养模式，致力于培养语言功底扎实、专业知识深厚、实践能力过硬的具有中国情怀和国际视野的复合型国际事务人才。他们既是学院的教学骨干，又是科研的中坚力量，朝气蓬勃，奋发进取，积极关注复合型国际化人才培养的前沿问题。

感谢学校领导对教材出版的大力支持，感谢时事出版社领导对教材编写的鼎力相助，特别是谢琳主任及其团队对教材的悉心审阅和设计建议。同时，还要感谢四川外国语大学国际关系学院师生团队对教材编写所付出的辛勤努力。

我们衷心希望，本系列特色教材能够充实国家和地方教育行政部门、高等院校和其他教育机构的资料库，继续提高学校的国际化水平，进而为培养复合型国际化人才贡献更大的力量！

四川外国语大学国际关系学院院长

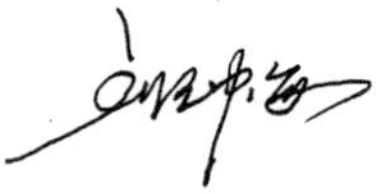

前言

Preface

随着中国改革开放的不断深入，中外之间的文化交流和商务往来日趋频繁，涉外工作已经揭去那层神秘的面纱，再也不是外事部门的“专利”，而是已经深入各个领域、各个部门和各个单位。在改革开放40余年各行各业取得辉煌成就的今天，中国在国际上的威望和作用日渐显著，世界经济一体化的形势促使我们必须强化国际交流的地位和角色。在这纷繁复杂的交往中，外交外事文书的应用和写作尤显重要。外交、外事和外商事业的发展，必然要求涉外文体写作与之相适应。可是，近些年来，我国出版了大量应用写作教材、专著，唯独缺少外交文体写作方面的著述，这不能不说是一种遗憾。为了适应中国当前改革开放的新形势，满足涉外工作空前繁荣的需要，给各行业、各系统、各部门的涉外交往工作提供方便，我们特地组织人员编写了《外交外事文书写作》一书。

《外交外事文书写作》收集整理了使用于国家与国家之间，或国家与联合国等国际组织之间进行国际联络和外事活动的专用文书。全书共8章，覆盖了外交外事文书写作的各个主要应用场合，具体包括国事文书、社交文书、讲演文书、告启文书、规约文书、商务文书等。本书在编写过程中注意吸收当前最新的理论知识和成果，体例上力求在前人研究的基础上有所创新，每章首先进行“内容概览”，概述该类文书的概念、分类、性质、特点、作用和写作要求；“基础知识”部分仅对相关理论和写作要求做简明扼要的介绍，以够用为准；“案例分析”方面，尽量贴近主题，所给示例均为中国外交场合正式文稿，极具参考价值。

分析环节突出重点、析透难点；“拓展阅读”为学习者提供与该章内容密切相关的权威中英文阅读材料，并且附上思考练习，促进学习者有效吸收消化本章内容；“课后练习”选材精炼、针对性强，能达到让学习者举一反三、灵活运用的目的。另外，根据文书写作必须具备实用性的特点，在练习中增加了情景模拟环节，引导学习者通过各种虚拟场景了解和掌握各章内容，以便能在外交外事文书的写作中游刃有余，恰到好处地处理各种不同类型的写作实践。

本书有利于扩大学习者的英语词汇量，提高其用英语撰写的基本能力，进而提升学习者的英文水平；简单易懂的基础理论搭配形式多样的案例，有助于训练学习者的思辨能力和案例分析能力；题型丰富的课后练习题可以进一步夯实学习者的基础知识，培养多元化的外事外交技能技巧。本书具有以下几方面的突出特点：

语言的实用性。为适应外交外事交流的客观需求，全书力求用中英文双语讲解。所选取的案例、拓展阅读材料以及课后练习均强调英语所占比重，以培养学习者灵活运用两种语言的能力。

资料的权威性。各种外交外事文书的写作技巧、方法和参考范例，诸如不同外交场合的祝酒词、讲演稿、贺电、邀请函等都可以在本书中找到。书中还列举了大量具有实践意义的经典案例。

内容的现代性。书中所编撰的内容尽量与现实紧密结合，范例大多是目前实际生活中正在运用的，尤其是中国不断融入国际进程，与国际政治经济接轨后的写作技巧与范例。

《外交外事文书写作》是在四川外国语大学国际关系学院的通盘统筹和具体策划下编写的，自始至终离不开时事出版社工作人员的关照和指导，在本书付梓之际，谨向他们表示深深的谢意。本书在编写过程中得到马彦、梁诗闻、贾思梅三位同学的大力支持，在此感谢他们付出的辛勤劳动。

在编写过程中，我们参考借鉴了国内外有关教材和研究成果、网络资料，吸取了其中许多有益的内容，在此不再一一列举，谨向有关作者表示深切的谢意。尽管付出了极大的努力，但由于我们水平有限、时间仓促，这其中肯定会有这样那样的不足，万望同仁和专家批评指正，以便进一步修改完善。

目录

Contents

5 Documents of Declaration

6 Documents for Stipulations and Agreements

7 Documents for Commercial Affairs

8 Notes for Classical Chinese Writings

Recommendations

1 Introduction to Documents of Foreign Affairs
第一章 外交外事文书概述

Abstract

Documents for foreign affairs are a style of writing aimed at dealing with affairs related to diplomatic and other fields. According to their application, they can be categorized into documents for national affairs, social occasions, speeches, notification, stipulation and business.

Documents for foreign affairs are characterized by distinctive features, including the seriousness of the formulating authority, qualifications of writing objects, restrictiveness of the language, complexity of the writing process and normalization of the writing procedure. They exert the functions of stipulation, notification and certification in a country's foreign activities.

Generally, the writing of documents for foreign affairs goes through preparation, drafting and revision, during which special attention should be paid to the format, person, salutation, complementary remarks and words, etc.

内容概览

作为涉外文书的一类，外交外事文书是一国处理有关外交事务的写作文体。根据应用场合及目的，外交外事文书主要分为国事文书、社交文书、演讲文书、告启文书、规约文书和商务文书几大类。

外交外事文书特点鲜明，其撰制权力具有严肃的国家性、撰制对象具有严格的限定性、撰制语言具有明确的限制性、撰制过程具有超乎寻常的复杂性、撰制程序具有明显的规范性，在一国对外活动中发挥了规约、知照与凭证的作用。

撰写外交外事文书一般要经过准备、起草与修改三个阶段，在撰写的过程中要特别注意格式、人称、称呼、客套用语和文字等几方面的要求。

(Rana, 2011)

The Definition and Types of Documents for Foreign Affairs

Definition

Document for foreign affairs is a general term for the working papers closely related to foreign affairs. It is used in various fields, such as state visits, negotiations, entry into treaty, international conference and organizations. Concerning political, economic, military, scientific and cultural relationship between countries or countries and international organizations, it reflects a formal sense of politics and policies.

(Berridge & Lloyd, 2012)

1.1 Definition and Types
第一节 外交外事文书的含义及种类

一、外交外事文书的含义

外交外事文书是涉外部门和涉外工作者处理与外交工作有密切关系的、日常性的事务工作文体的总称。具体来说，它是国家元首、政府首脑、外交部和外交代表机关等，为实行一国对外政策，进行外交活动，诸如访问、谈判、交涉、缔结条例、参加国际会议和国际组织等，所形成和使用的文件材料。各国的外交外事文书均体现了本国的对外方针政策和有关法规。它的内容总是涉及国家之间、国家与国际组织之间的政治、经济、军事、科学文化等各种关系，因此是国家间一种政治性、政策性很强的文书。

（辛业江，1990）

外交外事文书的含义有广义和狭义之分。从狭义上讲，外交外事文书特指国家间的“书信往来”，主要包括照会、函件和备忘录等。从广义上讲，外交外事文书也称对外文书，是国家领导人、外交机关、外交代表及地方机关、军队、团体、企事业单位及法人在国际政治、外交、军事、经济贸易、科学文化、法律、宗教等实践活动中，发布和贯彻执行法律，证明身份，叙述事实，申述立场、观点，表明态度，交涉问题，传递信息，建立友谊，加强合作，通知事务，通告情况，订立协议，礼仪往来等的一种重要的书面表述工具。

Types

According to the application and purpose, documents for foreign affairs can be classified as follows:

1. Documents for National Affairs.
2. Documents for Social Occasions.
3. Documents for Public Speaking.
4. Documents for Illustration.
5. Documents for Stipulations and Agreements.
6. Documents for Commercial Affairs.

二、外交外事文书的种类

根据应用场合及目的，外交外事文书主要分为以下几类：

1. 国事文书。
2. 社交文书。
3. 演讲文书。

4. 告启文书。
5. 规约文书。
6. 商务文书。

Features and Functions of Documents for Foreign Affairs

Features

1. The writing of documents for foreign affairs reflects solemnness of sovereignty.
2. The targeted content of documents for foreign affairs is strictly limited.
3. The language employed in documents for foreign affairs should be appropriately chosen.
4. The writing of documents for foreign affairs is extraordinarily complicated.
5. The procedure of writing documents for foreign affairs is highly standardized.

1.2 Features and Functions
第二节　外交外事文书的特点和作用

一、外交外事文书的性质与特点

外交工作具有高度的政治性、统一性、政策和策略性、组织纪律性，因此指导和记录外交活动的文书首先反映本国政府和人民的意志，是为本国外交政策服务的一种工具，其内容一般涉及国家、民族、一定的组织及法人的利益。所以，此类文书的文体格式、使用方式、撰制要求等都有一定的严肃性和国际通用的规范性。有了各种外交外事文书的写作，外交工作的情况可以上情下达，下情上报，左右沟通，使外交工作成为国家工作的有机组成部分。要想做好外交工作，离不开外交外事文书这个服务工具。

（周国宝、张慎霞，2005）

撰制外交外事文书与撰制普通文书大不相同，它具有自身独有的特点，主要体现在：

1. 外交外事文书的撰制权力具有严肃的国家性

这里的国家性有两层意思：一是外交外事文书具有典型的效力地域性特征，一国的文书没有经过另一国同意，是不能在另一国产生任何法律约束力的，这与内部使用的文书具有极大的差异；二是发文是国家政权发挥作用、行使国家行政职能的象征。

2. 外交外事文书的撰制对象具有严格的限定性

文书的撰制工作不是每个人都能进行的，对外交外事文书而言，其撰制对象更有严格的规定。作为国家外交政策、外交思想、外交行为的综合反映，外交外事文书的撰制受到统治者的严格控制。涉及具体部门事务的外交外事文书可以由具体部门去完成，但不能随心所欲，必须遵循严格的国家外交规则。以国家形式出现的外交外事文书，其最终的审定、批准权限属于最高统治者，属于国家最高决策层。

3. 外交外事文书的撰制语言具有明确的限制性

外交外事文书与内部文书的撰制不同，外交外事文书撰制的语言一般除选用本国的语言外，还应选用文书所涉及国的语言。除此之外，还应注意语言分寸得当，分清词语的程度深浅、范围大小、分量轻重、数量多少等，恰如其分地反映情况，说明问题，不说过头话等。要注意语言成分的完整性和词语搭配的规范性，避免滥用省略语。在修辞方法的选择上，可以适当使用引用、层递、对比等辞格，突出体现文书表达准确、严谨、简明、庄重的效果。

4. 外交外事文书的撰制过程具有超乎寻常的复杂性

外交外事文书是外交事务的载体，外交事务是复杂的，外交外事文书的撰制当然也是非常复杂的。外交事务涉及的时间长短不同，有的需要几年才能完成，有的需要几个月、几天完成，也有的要求瞬时完成。

这决定了外交外事文书撰制过程的复杂性。外交外事文书涉及双方或多方，要取得文书双方的认可，由草稿变成定稿，其过程也是复杂的。外交外事文书尤其是外交盟誓文书和国书，有时需要修改多遍才能最终完成。

5. 外交外事文书的撰制程序具有明显的规范性

程序性是文书工作的基本特性，程序性可以加快文书的整个处理过程，提高文书工作的效率。作为文书的一个门类，外交外事文书的撰制也具有明确的程序性。当然，外交外事文书的程序性与普通文书是有差异的，只有当一个完整程序结束时，外交外事文书的撰制才算完成。而这种撰制过程还包括文书的对外公布以及存档。

（冒志祥，2012）

Functions

Documents for foreign affairs can function in the following aspects:

1. As stipulations.
2. As illustrations.
3. As certificates.

二、外交外事文书的作用

随着中国对外政治、经济关系的加强和文化、教育、科学技术交流活动的频繁，外交外事文书的使用不仅在数量上有所增加，而且在文种上不断扩大，其重要作用也日益凸显出来。外交外事文书在国际交往中的主要作用体现为：

1. 规约作用

在外交外事文书中，有相当部分内容是用以规范和约束制文双方或各方的行为或行动的。如外交外事文书中的联合声明、宣言、公约、协定，以及国际会议所通过的决议等，均对参与各方具有平等的约束力。在经济、文化教育、科技往来中的协议、合同等，同样具有这种规约作用。在国际政治活动中，违约者不仅要承担政治责任，还要受到道义上的谴责。在经贸、文化往来活动中的违约者，不仅要承担道义责任，更要承担经济责任。

2. 知照作用

一般来说，各类外交外事文书都具有知照作用。一封信札，一纸电文，无论是道贺、致歉或是谴责，其最初的作用就是告知对方某事、某人或某物。外交外事文书中的告启类、说明类及书信中有关周知内容的信札，其制作目的就在于通知对方有关私务、公务等事宜。告启类文书除了知照目的外，还有解释的作用。

3. 凭证作用

对外交往中的各类文书应该说都具有存查凭证作用。无论是双向文书、多向文书或泛向文书（无明确接受对象的文书），一经制作发出，不管其质量优劣，或是内容上所涉及事务及人的重要程度，均不以人的主观意志为转移地产生一种凭证作用。文书的制作者可以此为据来协调有关各方关系。非关涉者，在需要时，也可随时依据有关文书与相关方面进行交往。有些文书的直接目的就是为了存查，如条据、契约等。

（段芹、丁金国，1994）

Writing Process and Requirements

Writing Process

The writing of documents for foreign affairs is composed of three phases: preparation, drafting, and revision.

1.3 Writing Process and Requirements
第三节 外交外事文书的撰写步骤和要求

一、关于外交外事文书撰写的一般说明

外交外事文书是国际往来的书信形式，包括照会、外交函件、备忘

录、国书、电报、证书、条约、公报和声明等，是进行对外交涉和礼仪往来的一种重要手段，也是外交业务的重要组成部分。外交外事文书体现国家的外交方针、政策和有关法规，所以起草和发送外交外事文书是政策性很强的工作。外交外事文书要求文字严谨、精练、准确，印制整洁，格式规范。书写外交外事文书时既不能违背本国文字习惯，又要照顾到国际惯例和驻在国的具体情况。大致来说，要注意文书的格式、人称、客套语及文字等方面的规范。

二、外交外事文书的撰写步骤

1. 准备阶段

这是接受写作任务到起草文稿之间的工作，要抓好以下几个环节：

（1）明确意图。外交外事文书是遵命文章，每一份外交外事文书从内容到文种，都是由领导根据工作的需要而决定的。涉外秘书在接受撰写任务时，首先要认真领会领导意图，明确要解决什么问题，达到什么目的，这样才能写出符合领导意图的外交外事文书。

（2）收集材料。写作外交外事文书要实事求是，要根据写作意图收集材料。材料的来源一靠平日的积累，二靠调查研究，三靠查找文献资料。只有收集完整、有价值的材料，才能写出符合客观实际、有指导现实意义的文书。撰写外交外事文书切忌凭空臆断或道听途说，这样写出来的东西必然是空洞无物、无的放矢、毫无用处的。

（3）提炼主题。在领会领导意图，明确撰写目的的基础上，对收集的材料做一番去伪存真、去粗取精、由表及里的分析工作之后，便可以抓住本质的、核心的东西，逐渐形成外交外事文书的主题。

（4）布局抓纲。确定外交外事文书的主题之后，即可考虑如何组织材料去体现主题，从而进入“打腹稿”阶段，将中心思想、基本观点、主要材料、框架结构等合理地加以组合，谋篇布局，并且用文字记录下来，也就是列出写作提纲。写作提纲可长可短，需根据外交外事文书的内容、篇幅长短或个人写作习惯来决定。

2. 起草阶段

起草阶段就是撰稿人按照拟好的提纲，把考虑好的内容用语言文字表达出来，以形成文书初稿的阶段。这个阶段最好是按照拟好的提纲一口气写成，不要时断时续，打断写作的思路。按照有关规定，起草文书的基本要求是：

（1）要准确选用外交外事文书文种，严格按选定的文种进行写作。

（2）根据本单位的隶属关系和职权范围行文。

（3）草拟文书应当做到：第一，符合国家的方针、政策和法律、法规及有关规定。第二，情况属实、观点明确、条理清楚、文字精练、书写工整、标点准确，篇幅力求简短。第三，人名、地名、数字、引文准确。第四，必须使用国家标准计量单位。第五，用词用字准确、规范。文内使用简称，一般应当先用全称，并注明简称。

（4）文书中的数字，除成文时间、部分结构层次序数和词、词组、惯用语、缩略语、具有修辞色彩语句中作为词素的数字必须使用汉字外，应当使用阿拉伯数字。

（5）草拟以及修改、签批文书，用笔用墨必须符合存档要求，不得在文稿装订线上书写。

3. 修改阶段

初稿的写作只是文书撰写过程中的一个阶段。初稿完成之后，还需要反复推敲修改才能定稿。

首先，撰稿人修改。撰稿人对复杂事务有一个认识的过程，草拟大纲时虽然曾经过反复考虑，但“智者千虑，必有一失”，文稿草拟后回过头来看，还会有不足的地方，这就需要一遍一遍地加工与修改，直到自己满意为止。“文章不厌百回改”，首先要自己修改好，不要依赖别人。修改时先要着眼于外交外事文书的内容，考虑主题是否得到明确表达，是否做到了主题与材料统一等，然后从篇章结构、文字表达、语法修辞等方面进行推敲。修改完毕后，要将全文通读一遍，再交由办公室修改。

其次，办公室修改。这是由办公室主任或资深的秘书进行审核的阶段。审核的重点是：是否符合国家的方针、政策和法律、法规及有关规定，是否要与有关部门协商，文字表述、文种使用、文书格式等是否符合有关规定。

最后，领导人修改、签发，这是最后把关的阶段。领导人经过认真审阅，把发现的问题改正过来，即可签发。一旦签发，即表明领导人对这份文书负完全责任，这份文书也就此生效。所以，领导人在审核文书时必须以极端负责的精神，精益求精，慎之又慎，容不得半点马虎。

Requirements

Several aspects should be paid much attention to, including format, person, addressing, honorific and the choice of words.

三、外交外事文书的撰写要求

在撰写外交外事文书的过程中，要特别注意以下几方面的要求。

1. 格式

使用外交外事文书首先要注意格式，不要用错。如外长和外交代表使用正式照会，不要用普通照会的格式。非外交代表机构不要用照会格式，而应使用外交函件。

2. 人称

人称要与文书格式相适应。正式照会、外交函件、电报均以签署人的名义用第一人称写成。在正式照会中，一般不用“我们”一词，普通照会一般以单位名义用第三人称写成，称对方亦用第三人称。以机构名义书写的对外函件亦用第三人称。

3. 称呼

外交外事文书抬头即受文人的职衔、姓名及单位名称等要全称，文中第一次出现时亦用全称，此后可用简称。对外交外事文书中受文人的身份称呼，部长级以上官员和大使、公使级使节一般称“阁下”（有些国家习惯用“先生”，不称“阁下”），如果受文人有爵位、学位或其他头衔，可依习惯称呼。

4. 客套用语

客套用语与格式相适应。以照会为例，普通照会开头的“××向××致意”这一客套用语不能用作个人函件中的开始语，非外交机关发送的外交外事文书亦不用这一套语，照会结尾的致敬语要与双方的身份、关系和场合相适应。致敬语一般用“顺致最崇高的敬意”“顺致崇高的敬意”“顺致敬意”。致外交部和大使馆的照会，一般可用“最”字；但事务性的照会和致代办（指代办处）的照会，不用“最”字。致敬语不能自成一页，应紧跟正文后另起一段。

5. 文字

外交外事文书一般以本国文字为正本，同时附有收件国文字或国际通用文字的译文。按照有关规定，我国政府及驻外外交代表机构发出的正式外交外事文书一律使用中文，同时附以驻在国文字或国际通用文字的译文。一般事务性函件可只用驻在国文字或在驻在国通用的外国文字。

（王保华、齐明敏、张宏，2002）

问题与思考

1. 什么是外交外事文书？外交外事文书可以分为哪几类？
2. 外交外事文书有哪些特点？主要能够发挥哪些作用？
3. 怎样撰写外交外事文书？有哪些方面需要注意？

2 Documents for National Affairs

第二章 国事文书

Abstract

The modern times have strengthened the relations between individual countries and between countries and international organizations. Documents for national affairs serve as the carrier of information exchange at the national level. They are usually passed from a national government to its counterpart formally, to convey the information about diplomatic relations.

According to different application areas and objectives, documents for national affairs fall into three categories: letter of credence, note and memorandum. The three types of documents will be brought into full account in terms of their definition, functions and contents, to understand their various application areas and objectives. The selected bilingual case studies aim to enhance understanding of the three documents and to promote writing skills through practices.

内容概览

时代的发展使得国家之间、国家和国际组织之间有了更频繁的联系。国家层面的信息互通主要以国事文书作为载体。国事文书作为一种正式的文书形式，通常由一国政府提交给另一国政府，传递有关国事交往信息。

依照不同的应用领域和目的，国事文书可分为国书、照会和备忘录。本章详细介绍了三种国事文书的定义、作用和内容，并明确了它们的使用场合及目的。本章以精选的案例分析作为范本，旨在从正反两方面加强读者对三种文书的理解，并通过实战演练提高相关人员关于这三种文书的写作水平。

2.1 Letter of Credence

第一节 国书

Basic Knowledge

一、基础知识

Introduction

A letter of credence is a formal letter usually sent by one head of state to another head of state that formally grants diplomatic accreditation to a named individual (usually but not always a diplomat) to be the sending country's ambassador in the receiving country.

Letters of credence are presented personally to the receiving head of state by ambassador-designates in a formal ceremony. Letters of credence are also referred to as "credentials", and the ambassador is said to be "presenting his credentials".

When two countries maintain relations at the chargé level, the letter of credence will be written by the foreign minister of the sending state, and addressed to the foreign minister of the receiving state. The chargé will also formally present his credentials to the foreign minister.

（一）简介

所谓的国书（英文是 letter of credence 或 credential），它并不是一本

书，而是国际交往中的一种全权证书。当一个国家向另一个建交国家派遣常驻全权代表（如大使）时，该国的国家元首要给派驻国的国家元首签署一封介绍信，这封介绍信就叫“国书”。它的目的是请求接收国给予该国的大使个人以外交信任。

（宗学军，2005）

大使就任国书一式两份，一个正本，一个副本。正本密封，副本开封。正本由派遣国元首签署，外交部长副署，由使节亲自向驻在国元首递交；副本则印上国家元首、外交部长的签名，不签署。国书由任使馆馆长的大使或公使前往已对人选表示同意的接受国赴任时携带，大使到达驻在国以后，应及时将副本呈送驻在国外交部长，系通知到达之意，并提出向贵国元首递交正本的愿望。密封的正本是觐见时大使亲手交给驻在国元首的国书。

（潘新明，1984）

国书的作用如下：在一国元首或他（她）的代表者正式接受国书之前，一个提名的大使是不能享受包括外交豁免权在内的外交人员的身份的，即这位大使在法律上还不能算是已就任的大使，不能以大使身份进行正式的官方活动，也不能正式履行职务，由此足见国书对于大使的重要性。

（宗学军，2005）

Contents and Features

Credentials can be classified according to either contents or foreign relations.

Based on contents, credentials fall into letter of dispatch and letter of recall. Comparatively, according to levels of foreign relations, credentials may be written by officials of different levels.

Until a head of state or his or her delegate formally accepts a letter of credence, an ambassador-designate does not formally assume diplomatic status, including the possession of diplomatic immunity.

A letter of recall means the opposite; it's a letter sent from one head of state to another head of state recalling an ambassador, either as a means of diplomatic protest or because the diplomat is being reassigned elsewhere and is being replaced by another envoy.

（二） 内容和特点

按照使用内容，国书可分为派遣国书和召回国书。

1. 派遣国书（letter of dispatch）

一般单独提及国书时，都指“派遣国书”。派遣国书亦称为就任国书，是一国元首派遣本国的使节前赴另一国行使外交任务的信任状，也是向接使国介绍所派使节情况的介绍信。

（阎泽川，2013）

2. 召回国书（letter of recall）

召回国书亦称辞任国书，它同样是由一国元首签名，外交部长副署，向另一国元首说明召回其使节原因的文书。除因国交断绝等原因外，召回国书一般措辞都比较热情、客气。

召回国书一般由被召回的使节在辞别觐见时递交给驻在国元首，如果使节早已离开了该国，则由继任者在递交就任国书时同时递交。有的国家在外交实践中，近年来已将继任使节的派遣国书和前任使节的召回国书合并为一个国书，只在国书中加一句“接替前任”的话，这是精简文书的一项措施。

（潘新明，1984）

一般而言，国书的特点包括如下几方面：

1. 它是缺乏国事访问的国家之间交流的最正式的方式，所采用的题目和风格都相当正式，所以它所使用的语言必须是正式、规范的。

2. 现今外交关系中所使用的国书大都行文简洁，篇幅短小，虽然各国国书有各自的格式，但实质都是相似的，言简意赅。

Writing Requirement

The writing of credentials should be brief and adhere to format requirements. Different countries may employ various ways and formats in writing credentials, but three parts may be generally found in all credentials: heading, content and signature.

（三）写作要求

国书的写作要简短，而且有一定的格式：要载明使节的姓名、官职与特别头衔、派遣目的、行使的权利，并赞赏该使节的忠实可靠、卓越才华、工作能力，表示希望保持同对方国家的友好关系，请求对方国家元首对该使节给予优厚待遇，对以本国元首或政府的名义所通知的事项给予信任，工作给予方便、支持和协助等。最后，需要派遣国的国家元首亲笔签署，并由外交部长副署。

（金伯雄，2002）

国与国之间的国书格式有所不同，但各国国书记载的事项均类似，一般有抬头、内容、署名三部分。

1. 抬头（heading）

×××国总统×××阁下

2. 内容（content）

内容包括：外交代表的任命及其等级，该使节代表本国元首或政府的言行，请驻在国国家元首予以信任等。当下，为了方便起见，可以将派遣国书与召回国书合并，只需在最后附上“××大使，现予召回，表达对驻在国在前大使任职期间接待和帮助的感谢”就行。

3. 署名（signature）

中华人民共和国主席（签字）

中华人民共和国外交部长（签字）（副署）

×年×月×日于北京

国字第×××号

Case Studies
二、案例分析

（一）召回国书

Field-Marshal Mohammed Aybu Khan
President of the Republic of Pakistan
to His Excellency
The Chairman of the People's Republic of China

GREAT AND GOOD FRIEND,

Dr. A. M. Malik who has for some time been the Ambassador Extraordinary and Plenipotentiary of Pakistan, having been recalled, and being unable to present his Letter of Recall in person, I have entrusted to his successor the duty of placing it in Your Excellency's hands.

I am confident that Dr. A. M. Malik, during his mission, devoted all his efforts to the promotion of understanding and goodwill and to the strengthening of friendly relations existing between our two countries, and I entertain the hope that while fulfilling satisfactorily the trust reposed in him he succeeded in gaining Your Excellency's esteem and goodwill.

Given at President's House, Karachi, this 1st 3 day of August in the year One Thousand and Nine Hundred and Sixty One.

Your Good Friend

SD/ M. A. Khan

（文献来源：黄金祺编:《英汉对照外交文献文书教程》（下册），世界知识出版社2004年版，第185页。）

Analysis

The heading of the letter of credence signifies the relationship between source country and target country, namely, from "Pakistan" to "the People's Republic of China". After the appropriate addressing follows the body part which deals with recalling and the general assessment of the bilateral relations. Finally, signature is made after the date.

(二) 派遣国书

中华人民共和国中央人民政府主席致苏维埃社会主义
共和国联盟最高苏维埃主席团主席的国书
(1949 年 10 月 20 日)

苏维埃社会主义共和国联盟最高苏维埃主席团主席
史维尔尼克先生阁下：

中华人民共和国中央人民政府成立伊始，承苏维埃社会主义共和国联盟政府首先愿与我政府建立外交关系，中国人民对此极感欣慰。中华人民共和国中央人民政府热忱欢迎建立中华人民共和国与苏维埃社会主义共和国联盟之友好邦交，并坚信此种邦交的建立与巩固，不仅有利于贵我两国之亲密合作，抑且有利于世界和平与安全。为此，本政府特任命王稼祥为驻贵国特命全权大使，并令其向贵主席亲呈国书。希予延见，给以信赖。顺颂贵主席政躬康泰，贵国国家繁荣，人民兴旺。

中华人民共和国中央人民政府毛泽东
外交部部长周恩来
一九四九年十月二十日北京

国字第一号

（文献来源：廉正保、王景堂、黄韬鹏：《解密外交文献——中华人民共和国建交档案（1949－1955）》，中国画报出版社2006年版，第26－27页。）

分析概要

同召回国书一样，派遣国书的抬头也需要表明国书来源国与目标国的关系，即由“中华人民共和国”向“苏维埃社会主义联盟”陈述相关事宜。在称呼方面，要加上对方的职位。在正文中，除了清楚表明新任大使的名称之外，还要展望两国关系的发展前景并以致敬语结束。最后部分是署名和日期。

Supplementary Readings
三、拓展阅读

请阅读以下两则国书并回答相应的问题。

Kuo Tzu No. 185

Chairman Liu Shao-chi of the People's Republic of China to His Excellency Kenneth Kaunda, President of the Republic of Zambia

Your Excellency,

For the purpose of establishing and developing the friendly relations and cooperation between the People's Republic of China and the Republic of Zambia, I have, in accordance with the decision of the Standing Committee of the National People's Congress of the People's Republic of China, appointed Mr. Chin Lichen Ambassador Extraordinary and Plenipotentiary of the People's Republic of China to the Republic of Zambia.

I request your Excellency to receive him favourably and give full credence to all of that he may represent to your Excellency in the name of the

Government of the People's Republic of China.

（文献来源：黄金祺编：《英汉对照外交文献文书教程》（下册），世界知识出版社 2004 年版，第 179 页。）

Reading Comprehension

Directions: Please give brief answers to the following questions.

1. What are the source country and target country of the credential respectively?
2. Can you generalize some basic features of the above credential?
3. Are there, if any, deficiencies in both content and structure of the above credential?
4. What is your idea to improve the above credential?

苏维埃社会主义共和国联盟最高苏维埃主席团致
中华人民共和国中央人民政府主席的国书（译文）
（1949 年 10 月 3 月）

苏维埃社会主义共和国联盟最高苏维埃主席团（致）
中华人民共和国中央人民政府主席毛泽东先生

主席先生：

苏维埃社会主义共和国联盟最高苏维埃主席团，切望始终不渝地促进巩固苏维埃社会主义共和国联盟与中华人民共和国间所如此幸福地建立起之友好关系，并深信巩固苏中之间的友谊，符合和平与国际安全之利益，因此，决定任命公民尼古拉·瓦西里维奇·罗申为驻贵国特命全权大使。

苏维埃社会主义共和国联盟最高苏维埃主席团授予公民尼古拉·瓦西里维奇·罗申本国书，请您，主席先生，惠然赐见，并信赖其荣幸地代表苏维埃社会主义共和国联盟政府向您所陈述之一切。

什维尔尼克（签字）

苏联外交部副部长签署
葛罗米柯（签字）

莫斯科·克里姆林宫
一九四九年十月三日

（文献来源：廉正保、王景堂、黄韬鹏：《解密外交文献——中华人民共和国建交档案（1949－1955）》，中国画报出版社2006年版，第26－27页。）

Reading Comprehension

Directions: Please give brief answers to the following questions.

1. 这是中华人民共和国接收到的第几份国书？
2. 该封国书是在什么历史背景下诞生的？它有何历史意义？
3. 结合前几份国书，说说你对国书的格式和内容有了什么样的认识？

2.2 Note
第二节 照会

Basic Knowledge
一、基础知识

Introduction

The Note is the most commonly used form of written communication in diplomatic intercourse. Basically, there are two kinds of Notes: Formal Note (or

Official Note）and Verbal Note（or Note Verbal）.

A Formal Note is essentially a formal personal letter. It is the most formal form of written communication used between the foreign minister of one country and his counterpart in another, between a foreign minister and a head of mission or between one head of mission and another. It deals with comparatively more important political affairs or diplomatic formalities.

A Verbal Note is also a form of written communication and not an oral one as the term "Verbal" might indicate. The idea implicit in this term is that a Verbal Note once constituted a formal record of an oral communication or of a conversation.

（一）简介

照会是外交交往中最常见的文书形式，是国家和国家在相互对应的外交部及其派出的外交代表机关，以及外交代表之间的相互往来中，进行交涉时用于表明自己的立场、态度或通知事项等的一种常见的外交外事文书。

照会总体上分为正式照会和普通照会。

正式照会实质上是正式的个人函件，是外交外事文书中最正式的形式，一般用于外交部长之间、外交部长与使馆馆长之间、使馆馆长之间，用于处理较为重大的政治事务和外交礼仪。

普通照会也是一种外交外事文书，虽不如正式照会正式，但比正式照会使用频率更高、范围更广，既可以用来处理最重大的政治问题，又可以处理纯技术性的各种事务。

Contents and Features

A Formal Note is drafted in the first person. A Formal Note, as mentioned, is used to deal with comparatively more important affairs and diplomatic formalities, for example:

a. for a state to officially inform foreign governments of important events such as a change in its political system; change of state leaders; diplomatic recognition; establishment, severance or resumption of diplomatic relations; replacement of consuls.

b. to make representations on such issues as conclusion or revision of a treaty; convening of an international conference; the establishment of consulates on reciprocal terms; arrangements for visits of state leaders; other important political, military or economic affairs.

c. to fulfill such diplomatic formalities as transmitting important messages from a head of state or government; expressing congratulations or condolences; notifying the assumption of post by an ambassador, his departure or return.

d. any other matter for which a Formal Note is deemed necessary to stress its importance.

The Verbal Note is a third person Note used between diplomatic services of different countries, for instance, between one ministry of foreign affairs and another, between a ministry of foreign affairs and embassy, between one embassy and another, and so on. Though less formal, it is much more commonly used than a Formal Note. It can deal with a wide scope of affairs including political problems of the utmost importance to matters of purely technical nature. With the trend of simplifying formalities in diplomatic practice, a Verbal Note can now be used on many occasions which would otherwise require a Formal Note. In such cases, local usage, reciprocity and other factors should be taken into consideration in choosing which form of Note to use.

（二）内容和特点

1. 正式照会

正式照会主要涉及正式通知外国政府重大事情、就重大问题进行交涉或履行重大的外交礼仪，显示出对某一件事情特别重视，行文用第一人称。

2. 普通照会

普通照会可以用来处理从最重大的政治问题到纯技术性的各种事务，具体可以分为有关外交礼节的普通照会、杂务普通照会等。普通照会广泛用于外事部门之间，如外交部与外交部、外交部与使馆、使馆与使馆之间等，一般用第三人称行文。

（黄金祺，2004）

Writing Requirement

The Formal Note and the Verbal Note may follow different writing requirements. For the Formal Note, the first person should be used. In the addressing part, "Your Excellency" is used to address minister (or undersecretary) and ambassador, while "Mr. " is to address the Chargé d'affairs. For the Verbal Note, it is less formal than the Formal Note, but it is more widely used. Usually in the third person, it does not have the addressing part. Instead, it always begins and ends with words of salutation.

（三）写作要求

1. 正式照会（Formal Note）

（1）行文使用第一人称。

（2）称呼：对部长（副部长）和大使称"Your Excellency"（阁下），对代办称"Mr. ×"（×先生）。称呼置于照会正文之前。正文中需要称呼受文人时，部长或大使仍用"Your Excellency"或只用"You"（汉语习惯用"你"，不用您），代办则用"You"。

（3）致敬语：用于照会的结尾。汉语的致敬语已较简化，都只写作："顺致最崇高的敬意。"

2. 普通照会（Verbal Note）

（1）普通照会不如正式照会正式，但不一定不如正式照会重要。普通照会比正式照会用得更多，可以用来处理广泛的事务。（2）普通照会用第三人称。英语普通照会没有称呼，而是用致敬语开头和结尾。在正文之后是日期和发文地点以及外交部或使馆印章，最后是信尾。普通照会不用签字，但有些国家的普通照会注明起草人姓名的首字母。

注意：英语正式照会的日期放在右上角，而普通照会则放在下面。

（3）汉语普通照会仍用称呼（即受文机关的名称）而没有信尾。

Case Studies
二、案例分析

The Indian Ministry of External Affairs to the Chinese Embassy in New Delhi, 6 October 1962

The Ministry of External Affairs presents its compliments to the Embassy of the People's Republic of China and has the honour to refer to the note represented to the Chargé d'Affaires of India at the Peking on 3rd October, 1962.

The Government of India regret that the Chinese Government have not only turned down the proposal to hold further discussions regarding measures to remove the current tensions in the western sector, the implementation of which is a necessary preliminary to the creation of a climate of confidence between the two Governments for constructive discussions to resolve differences over the border question, but categorically have started that any consideration of measures for restoration of the status quo of the boundary unilaterally altered by force is absolutely unacceptable to the Chinese Government. How can any talks take place in the context of this precondition?

The Government of India have repeatedly stated their desire to enter into talks and discussions, first to devise measures to reduce tensions and to create a climate of confidence, and then to undertake purposeful and constructive discussions in the improved climate to resolve the differences between the two

Governments over the border question. The Government of India's approach in this matter of talks and discussions has been clear and straightforward-preliminary talks to ease tensions and to create the appropriate climate of confidence to be followed by further purposeful talks, after implementation of measures to ease tensions and restore confidence have been taken, to resolve differences between the two Governments on the boundary question on the basis of the report of the officials. If there has been any double dealing or hypocrisy, it is entirely on the Chinese side as can be seen in the succeeding four paragraphs below.

The Government of China have repeatedly stated in their communications sent to the Government of India that they have all along refrained from disturbing the status quo of the eastern sector of the boundary along the McMahon line, though they did not recognise it, as they were respecting the actualities of the situation. This boundary, running along the highest Himalayan watershed ridges, has been the traditional and customary boundary between India and Tibet for centuries and Indian administration bad been established right up to it. This was conclusively proved by the Indian officials at the talks of 1960. The Agreement of 1914—The McMahon Line Agreement—merely formalised the traditional boundary and gave it the added sanction of confirmation by treaty. The Government of China have recently accepted the eastern section of the McMahon line as the traditional watershed boundary between China and Burma. They have also in their recent publication, ‘Selected Documents on Sino-Indian Relations’, issued in 1962, attached a map showing the McMahon line as the alignment along ‘the Himalayan mountains’. This makes clear that even according to the Chinese, it was not just ‘a line which a Briton drew on a map at will without any basis’ but the highest watershed ridge in this area.

Despite this clear knowledge of the boundary, the Chinese forces have, during the last month, while notes were being exchanged for holding talks and discussions, intruded into Indianterritory in the eastern sector and have been attacking Indian forces since 20th September. The Government of India have in their notes of 17th, 21st, 25th and 28th September given full details of this unwarranted and deliberate Chinese violation of the status quo of the border. The Government of India in their note of 25th September requested the Government of China, in the light of the full details given by them regarding this latest intrusion of Chinese forces into Indian territory, to issue immediate instruction to their forces to cease their aggressive activities on Indian territory and to return to Chinese territory across the frontier to the north of the Thagla Ridge, i. e. , to the region indicated by the co-ordinates given by the Chinese authorities themselves in their note of 16th September, 27°49′ N and 91°48′ E. The Government of China have not only not taken any action in this regard, continued their aggressive activities in Indian territory and created further tensions in the Eastern sector, which has so far been quiet and peaceful, but are now arguing, on the basis of tensions created by their deliberate aggression, that the eastern sector being the most pressing question at present, should also be discussed. The Government of India will not enter into any talks and discussions under duress or continuing threat of force. The latest Chinese intrusion must be terminated first.

The Government of India in their note of 19th September commented on the suggestion of the Chinese Government regarding withdrawal of forces on both sides by 20 kilometers that this suggestion "suffers from the serious defect that it leaves the aggressor who altered the status quo by unilateral action over the last few years in possession of the fruits of his aggression". This comment of the Government of India is fully justified. While India has never altered the traditional status quo of the boundary, it is obviously the Chinese practice to alter the status quo unilaterally whenever they can. This has been further confirmed by the latest action of the Chinese forcesduring last month in the eastern sector. Quite apart from the claims of either side, it is clearly established that Chinese forces have, during the last month, crossed the Thagla Ridge and entered into the area on the Indian side. This cannot be denied. And further, they are continually strengthening their position on the Indian side of the Ridge. The Chinese forces have thus advanced into and occupied Indian territory. These facts are clear and no-one can be deceived by suggestions for talks and discussions and professions of peaceful settlement when force is actually being employed to grab Indian territory even while these notes for talks and discussions are being exchanged.

Nor can anyone be deceived by the false allegation that the Government of India have raised the question in such a way as to bog down the two sides in endless procedural debate and make it utterly impossible to start discussions on the boundary question. The position of the Government of India in this matter is clear as stated in the third paragraph above. It is the Government of China, on the other hand, that want to bog down the talks in endless debates and wrangles by proposing that neither side should refuse to discuss any questions concerning the Sino-Indian boundary that may be raised by the other side. No useful talks and discussions can take place in the absence of precise agenda and it appears that the Chinese are specifically aiming at creating confusion regarding the proposal for starting talks and discussions merely as a cover for their aggressive and expansionist activities along the India-China border.

The Government of India are prepared to make necessary arrangements for starting discussions in Peking or in Delhi from a mutually convenient date as soon as the latest intrusion by Chinese forces in Indian territory south of the McMahon line has been terminated as requested in Government of India's note of 25th September 1962, and the Chinese Government indicate their acceptance of the proposal made in thatnote, which is reproduced below for ready reference:

"The Government of India are prepared to hold further discussions at the appropriate level to define measures to restore the status quo in the Western sector which has been altered by force in the last few years and to remove the current tensions in that area. The implementation of such measures will create a climate of confidence between the two Governments which alone can make possible constructive discussions to resolve the differences between the two Governments on the boundary question on the basis of the report of the officials."

The Ministry of External Affairs avails itself of this opportunity to renew to the Embassy of the People's Republic of China the assurances of its highest consideration.

（文献来源：黄金祺编：《英汉对照外交文献文书教程》（上册），世界知识出版社2004年版，第117－121页。）

Analysis

In terms of the style of narration, this note belongs to verbal type, since it leads directly to body after heading, without addressing. Meanwhile, the third person is used in the note. According to structure, the heading indicates the bilateral relations between source country and target country, which is from "Indian Foreign Ministry" to "Chinese Embassay in New Deli". After the date that follows heading, the body first clarifies the purpose of this note, then narrates the background, mutual attitudes and expectations towards future. The note ends with complementary remarks towards the target country.

中国外交部给印度驻华大使馆照会
（一九六二年十月三日）

印度驻华大使馆：

中华人民共和国外交部向印度驻华大使馆致意，并且就印度政府一九六二年九月十九日照会申述如下：

一、中国政府对印度政府又一次提出的迅速和无条件地在两国官员报告的基础上讨论中印边界问题的建议，表示遗憾。

二、印度政府还拒绝了中国政府再次提出的双方武装部队沿边境全线各自后撤二十公里的建议，印度政府这样做的目的是很清楚的。印度方面利用中国边防部队停止边境巡逻的情况，从今年六月起又一次越过所谓麦克马洪线，侵入线北中国西藏地方扯冬、线不去、扯果布、卡龙四个侵略据点。双方各自后撤二十公里的建议，显然有碍于印度方面不仅在西段和中段，而且在东段进行这种侵略活动。印度政府一方面在九月十九日向中国发出照会，拒绝中国通过谈判和平解决边界问题的建议；另一方面从九月二十日起向扯冬地区的中国边防部队发动了连续攻击，截至九月三十日，共打死中国边防人员五人，打伤九人。这种猖狂的挑衅和攻击直到现在还没有停止。事实很清楚，印度政府决心要用枪炮来回答中国政府的和平建议，中国政府对此，不能不表示极大的愤慨。

三、印度政府来照中煞有介事地重复说：一定要缓和边境的紧张局势，才能讨论边境问题。这是彻头彻尾的虚伪。难道印度军队越过所谓麦克马洪线向中国边防人员开枪，这就是印度缓和边境紧张局势的努力吗？印度要进攻，中国一定要回击。印度政府必须承担由此而引起的一切严重后果。一方面说什么要缓和边境紧张局势，才能举行边界问题的讨论；另一方面却在边境上不断制造紧张局势，使边界问题越来越复杂，空洞的言辞骗不了任何人，蓄意持续用武力片面改变边界状况的行动决不会为印度带来任何好处。

四、中国政府是本着缓和边境紧张局势的诚意，再一次提出双方各自后撤二十公里的建议的。但是，印度政府来照却说这个建议有着“严重的缺陷”，“它使在过去几年中以片面行动改变了现状的侵略者得以据有侵略的果实”。事实上，不仅是几年来而是十多年来，用武力来片面改变边界状况的，恰恰是印度自己，关于西段和中段，中国政府在过去的历史照会中已经做了详尽的叙述。现在谈东段，中国再一次强调指出，所谓麦克马洪线是完全非法的，中国政府决不承认。事实上，这条线一直到一九五〇年中国和平解放西藏时止，还仅仅是一个英国人在一张地图上没有任何根据地任意画出来的一条线；它没有任何法律价值，也没有实际价值。印度方面只是在中国解放西藏后才片面地用武力改变了东段地区的传统习惯线，把边防部队推进到所谓麦克马洪线。印度政府不以此为满足，又在一九五九年侵占了所谓麦克马洪线以北的兼则马尼，又侵占了扯冬地区。所有这些，都是印度方面用武力改变边界状况的确凿事实。

五、中国政府一直抗议印度在边界西段、中段和东段用武力片面改变边界状况的行为，但是中国政府从中印两国人民的利益出发，从不提出恢复边界原状作为中印谈判边界问题的条件。中国政府的态度过去如此，现在仍然如此。亚洲国家和爱好和平的国家，都不难从这一点看出，中国政府是诚心诚意地致力于和平解决中印边界问题的。但是，印度政府却在来照中坚持边界问题的讨论要有先决条件，那就是，必须首先恢复中印边界西段印度心目中的所谓边界状况，即中国从自己的大片地区撤退，然后才能讨论中印边界问题。这是中国政府绝对不能同意的。看来很清楚，印度政府之所以这样提出问题，是为了使双方在来往照会中对程序性问题陷入无休止的争论，而使边界问题的讨论根本无从开始。

六、中国政府反对中印边界问题的讨论有任何先决条件，但是中国政府并不反对在讨论中印边界问题的过程中，讨论印度方面可能提出来的问题，印度来照说，只讨论西段边界的某些问题，为什么只讨论西段呢？东段的问题是当前最紧张的问题，有什么理由不去讨论它？中国政府现在再一次建议，两国政府在双方官员报告的基础上，立即开始中印边界问题的讨论；在讨论的过程中，既讨论关于西段边界问题，也必须讨论关于中段和东段边界问题。

七、关于具体的安排，中国政府注意到印度政府已经同意从十月十五日起在北京、后在德里轮流进行讨论的建议。中国政府准备在十月十五日接待印度方面派出的代表。中国政府并建议立即通过外交途径商定其他有关细节。

中国政府等待印度政府的答复

顺致最崇高的敬意。

中华人民共和国外交部

一九六二年十月三日于北京

（文献来源：《中华人民共和国对外关系文件集——第九集》，世界知识出版社 1964 年版，第 84－86 页。）

分析概要

从抬头看，这封照会由“中国外交部”向“印度驻华大使馆”发出。抬头的正下方是日期。从整体上看，该照会显得很正式。其一，在正文之前加上了称呼；其二，全文使用第一人称叙述。正文以向对方致意开始，将己方的诉求清楚的用数字番号标出，其间指出印度政府对争议地区的侵占以及我方的严正立场。照会最后以致敬语结束，其后是落款及日期。整封照会显得威严而不失礼节。

Supplementary Readings

三、拓展阅读

请仔细阅读以下两则照会的内容，回答问题。

中国外交部办公厅就王稼祥大使
赴任一事致苏联驻华使馆的照会（节选）
（1949 年 10 月 9 日）

敬启者，王稼祥大使暨随员一行十三人（内有苏联人二名——古早夫及阿洛夫同行）定于本月二十日下午五时由京出发，前赴莫斯科，惟因护照不及赶办，暂发给证明书，以便迅速成行。用特函请电达贵国政府分饬沿途关卡查照，准予以外交护照待遇为感。

专此顺颂

公祺此致

苏联大使馆

附上名单

外交部办公厅

主任王炳南

副主任阎宝航

一九四九年十月十九日

（文献来源：廉正保、王景堂、黄韬鹏主编：《解密外交文献——中华人民共和国建交档案（1949－1955）》，中国画报出版社2006年版，第22页。）

Reading Comprehension

Directions: Please give brief answers to the following questions.

1. 请说明该照会的来源国与目标国。
2. 请简述该照会的主要内容。
3. 从格式上看，该照会是否符合要求？有无需要补充的地方？
4. 从内容上看，该照会是否完整？能否达到有效传递信息的目的？

To Notify the Ratification of an Agreement

No.

The Ministry of Foreign Affairs of the People's Republic of China presents its compliments to the Embassy of and has the honour to inform the latter that on the President of the People's Republic of China ratified the "Agreement on Between the Government of."

The Ministry of Foreign Affairs requests the Embassy to convey the information to the Government of (or its Government).

The Ministry of Foreign Affairs avails itself of this opportunity to renew to the Embassy the assurances of its highest Consideration.

(Seal)

Place, date

Embassy of.
BEIJING.

（文献来源：黄金祺编：《英汉对照外交文献文书教程》（上册），世界知识出版社2004年版，第110页。）

Reading Comprehension

Directions: Please give brief answers to the following questions.

1. In terms of format, does this Note meet the requirement? Is there any place that needs revision?
2. Based on contents, is the Note complete? Has it attained the objective of transmitting information effectively?

2. 3 Memorandum
第三节 备忘录

Basic Knowledge
一、基础知识

Introduction

As indicated in the General Remarks of this Unit, Memorandum does not differ essentially from a Note, except that it doesn't begin and end with a formula of courtesy and it is less formal but more flexible than a Note.

A Memorandum is usually drafted in the third person, but it can also be in the first person.

1. With a view to avoiding misunderstanding, a Memorandum is prepared either before or after an interview as a formal record of the oral communication or conversation.
2. When a detailed statement of facts or a thorough expression of views or an elaborate argument on certain issues or such like is too long to be contained in a Note, a Memorandum is used, which can be as long as it is required.
3. Sometimes, a Memorandum is used as a polite reminder of a certain matter.

4. A Memorandum can also be used as a special form of agreement. It can be presented personally following an interview or delivered like a Note.

（一）简介

备忘录（也称节略，Memorandum 或 Aide-mémoire 或 Mémoire）实际上是口头通知或谈话的正式记录。它同照会没有实质性的区别，只是备忘录的起首和结尾不需要致敬语，也不需要签署。同普通照会一样，备忘录也可用于处理广泛的事务。它常用来详尽地陈述事实和观点。备忘录不如照会正式，但比照会灵活。备忘录一般用第三人称，但也有用第一人称的。

备忘录一般在下列情况下使用：

1. 为避免误解，使用备忘录作为一次会见时的口头通知或谈话的正式记录；这样的备忘录可以在会见之前就准备好，也可以在之后再补备。

2. 为了详细叙述某一事实，或就某一问题详尽陈述观点或论点，如果照会容纳不下即可使用备忘录；备忘录的篇幅可以视需要而定，是无限制的。

3. 有时，备忘录可用来作为客气的提醒和催询。

4. 备忘录也可用作一种特殊的协议形式，如谅解备忘录。

（黄金祺，2004）

Contents and Features

A Memorandum of some importance is usually marked with the title "memorandum" or "aide-mémoire", sometimes even with the subject of the communication. In the latter case, a Memorandum is often used for certain special purpose.

The kind of paper used in each case will depend upon the importance of the Memorandum concerned. For a Chinese Memorandum, the traditional rice paper is used. In the case of an important Memorandum, the paper bearing our national emblem is recommended.

（二）内容和特点

备忘录可按形式和内容分类。按形式分类，可分为面交备忘录、送交备忘录和谅解备忘录等；按内容分类，可分为说明性备忘录、纪要性备忘录、协议性备忘录和抗议性备忘录等。

备忘录的特点包括如下几方面：

1. 内容上的纪实性（fact-oriented）

备忘录，顾名思义，是记述其实，以备遗忘，供事后查对之用。

2. 写法上的灵活性（flexible in writing skills）

备忘录的格式、行文都比较灵活多样。比如说明具体事实的备忘录，很像说明文；条款式的备忘录，其写法像条约。

3. 表达的要点性（concisely focused）

备忘录撰写要围绕交往中涉及问题及对它的主要观点、意见和认同来整理、提炼和概括，切忌记流水账。

（郭英立，2012）

Writing Requirements

The writing of Memorandum is not completely same with other documents for foreign affairs. Generally, it is easy, including such parts as title, prologue, body, ending and signature.

Here are a few quick tips for writing effective memorandums:

1. Make sure that the body of the text is written in clear, concise and grammatically right language.
2. Do not use long and overly wordy sentences. Keep it simple.
3. Feel free to use bulleted lists and headings to convey your message.
4. Conclude the memo with any closing statements that may inspire the

recipient to take action.

5. Mention any and all attachments at the end of the memorandum by using the single word "Attachment."

（三）写作要求

备忘录和其他外交文件在写作上不完全一样，总的来说比较简单。具体来说，备忘录一般由标题、前言、正文、结尾、签章等部分组成。

1. 标题（title）

可以只写文种名称《备忘录》；可以由双方单位、事由和文种名称组成，如《中国××公司和德国××公司关于××技术转让问题的备忘录》；也可以由事由和文种名称组成，如《服装出口备忘录》；还可以由双方单位和文种名称组成，如《××大学和××集团备忘录》。有时，在标题下需要写明时间等。

2. 前言（prologue）

一般包括会谈双方单位名称及人员职衔，会谈的时间、地点、事由和内容；常用"双方达成如下谅解""达成协议如下"等惯用语引出下文。

3. 正文（body）

将洽谈中的主要问题或有争议的问题进行一一摘要记录，达成共识的要写其大意，存有差异的则要分别表达清楚各自的观点、意见及承诺。

4. 结尾（ending）

结尾写明该备忘录的生效期、份数、文本等。有时可以省略。

5. 签章（signature）

签署本备忘录的组织名称（盖章）和签署代表签字等。

Case Studies
二、案例分析

Memorandum Given by Indian Embassy in China to Chinese Ministry of Foreign Affairs October 21, 1950

The Central People's Governmentare fully aware of the views of the Government of India on the adjustment of Sino-Tibetan relations. It is, therefore, not necessary to repeat that their interest is solely in a peaceful settlement of the issue. My Government are also aware that the Central People's Government have been following a policy of negotiations with the Tibetan authorities. It has, however, been reported that some military action has taken place or is about to take place, which may affect the peaceful outcome of these negotiations.

Government of India would desire to point out that a military action at the present time against Tibet will give those countries in the world which are unfriendly to China a handle for anti-Chinese propaganda at a crucial and delicate juncture in international affairs. The Central People's Government must be aware that opinion in the United Nations has been steadily veering round to the admission of China into that organization before the close of the present session. The Government of India feel that military action on the eve of a decision by the Assembly will have serious consequences and will give powerfulsupport to those who are opposed to the admission of the People's Government to the United Nations and the Security Council.

At thc present time when international situation is so delicate any move that is likely to be interpreted as a disturbance of peace may prejudice the position of China in the eyes of the world. The Government of India's firm conviction is that one of the principal conditions for the restoration of a peaceful atmosphere is the recognition of the position of the People's Republic of China, and its association with the work of the United Nations. They feel that an incautious move at the present time even in a matter which is within itsown sphere will be used by those who are unfriendly to China to prejudice China's case in the United Nations and generally before neutral opinion. The Government of India attach the highest importance to the earliest settlement of the problem of Chinese representation in International Organizations and have been doing everything in their power to bring it to a successful conclusion. They are convinced that the position of China will be weakened if through military action in Tibet those who are opposed to China's admission are now given a chance to misrepresent China's peaceful aims.

The Government of India feel that the time factor is extremely important. In Tibet there is not likely to be any serious military opposition and any delay in settling the matter will not therefore affect Chinese interests, or a suitable final solution. Government of India's interest in this matter is, as we have explained before, only to see that the admission of the People's Government to the United Nationsis not again postponed due to causes which could be avoided and further that, if possible, a peaceful solution is followed where military action may cause unrest and disturbance on her own borders.

Indian Embassy in China

（文献来源：黄金祺编：《英汉对照外交文献文书教程》（上册），世界知识出版社 2004 年版，第 168－169 页。）

Analysis

In terms of structure, the memorandum is composed of title, prologue, body, ending and signature. The title indicates the origin and target countries, Indian Embassy in China and Chinese Ministry of Foreign Affairs. Below the title is the date, which then leads to the prologue, which concerns the background of India-Tibet relationship. The body narrates some regulations of

India-Tibet relationship and the conclusion puts forward hope for the future. The final part of memorandum is signature.

我致美国关于湖广铁路债券案的备忘录

（一九八三年二月二日）

中华人民共和国外交部谨就湖广铁路债券案申述如下：

（一）一九七九年十一月，美国公民杰克逊等九人在美国阿拉巴马州地方法院对中华人民共和国提起诉讼，要求偿还他们所持有的清政府于一九一一年发行的湖广铁路债券的本息。对此，中国政府曾多次照会美国国务院，提出交涉，申明中国根据国际法，享有主权豁免，不受任何外国法院审判；中国政府对历届反动政府的旧债概不承认，也不承担偿还的义务。但美国法院置中国政府的严正立场于不顾，竟然于一九八二年九月一日做出缺席判决，要求中国向原告偿还四千多万美元。美方甚至声称，如果中国政府对美国法院的判决置之不理，原告将要求美法院强制执上述判决，扣押中国政府在美国的财产。这就使问题发展到十分严重的地步。

（二）中国政府对于历届旧政府的外债一概不予承认，也不承担偿还的义务。这是我国政府的一贯立场。恶债不予继承是国际法久已公认的一项原则。在世界上，革命政权在推翻旧政权后对旧政权为维护其反动统治而借的外债不予偿还，也不乏先例。在半殖民地半封建的旧中国，帝国主义、封建主义、官僚资本主义给中国人民造成了深重的灾难。所谓湖广铁路债券，是丧权辱国的清朝政府，为维护其反动统治和镇压人民，勾结在华划分势力范围的帝国主义列强，加强压迫和掠夺中国人民的产物。对于这类旧外债，中国政府理所当然地不予承认。中国政府这一立场完全符合国际法原则，有充分的法理根据。

（三）国家主权豁免是国际法的一项重要原则，其根据是联合国宪章所确认的国家主权平等的原则。中国作为一个主权国家，无可非议地享有司法豁免权。美国地方法院对一个主权国家作为被告的诉讼，行使管辖权，做出缺席判决甚至以强制执行其判决相威胁，完全违反国家主权平等的国际法原则，违反联合国宪章。对于这一种将美国国内法强加于中国，损害中国主权、损害中国民族尊严的行为，中国政府坚决拒绝。如果美方无视国际法，强制执行上述判决，扣押中国在美国的财产，中国政府保留采取相应措施的权利。

（四）中国政府一贯主张在和平共处五项原则的基础上发展中美两国的关系。对湖广铁路债券案，中方从一开始就表明了自己的立场，要求美方做出妥善处理。但美国国务院却一直采取推卸责任的态度，致使事态发展到目前的地步。中国政府希望，美国政府切实负起责任，严格遵照国际法原则行事，采取积极步骤，制止事态发展，妥善处理此案，不使它给中美关系以及两国间正常的经济贸易往来造成损害。

中华人民共和国外交部
一九八三年二月二日于北京

（文献来源：黄金祺编：《英汉对照外交文献文书教程》（上册），世界知识出版社 2004 年版，第 166 – 167 页。）

分析概要

同英文备忘录相似，中文备忘录在结构上也包含了标题、正文、结尾和签章几部分。该备忘录的标题除了提到备忘录的来源国与目标国之外，还指明了主题，即关于“湖广铁路债券案”。标题下方是日期。与英文备忘录不同的是，该备忘录并无前言部分，而是开宗明义地进入有关“湖广铁路债券案”的申述正题，并以数字番号清楚地予以说明。结尾部分提出希望，最后是落款和时间。

Supplementary Readings

三、拓展阅读

请仔细阅读以下《中国大使馆给印度驻华大使馆的备忘录》的内容，回答问题。

中华人民共和国中央人民政府申明：西藏是中国领土不可分的一部分，西藏问题完全是中国的一个内政问题。中国人民解放军必须进入西藏，解放西藏人民，保卫中国边疆；这是中央人民政府的既定方针。中央人民政府曾屡次表示希望西藏问题能以和平谈判的方式得到解决，欢迎西藏地方代表团早日来北京，进行和平谈判。乃西藏代表团受人唆使，故意拖延来北京的行期，但中央人民政府仍未放弃与西藏地方当局进行和平谈判的愿望。可是无论西藏地方当局愿否进行和平谈判及谈判得到如何结果，均属中华人民共和国的内政问题，不容任何外国干预。

尤其是西藏问题与中华人民共和国进入联合国的问题，是两个完全没有关联的问题，如果那些对中国不友好的国家企图利用中华人民共和国中央人民政府对其领土西藏行使主权一事作为借口，进行威胁，以阻碍中华人民共和国进入联合国组织，那只是再一次表示这些国家对中国的不友好和敌对的态度而已。

因此，中华人民共和国中央人民政府对于印度政府所认为可悲叹的观点，不能不认为是受了西藏方面与中国敌对的外国势力的影响，而表示深切的遗憾。

（文献来源：西藏自治区党史资料征集委员会、西藏军区党史资料征集领导小组编：《和平解放西藏》，西藏人民出版社1995年版，第167－168页。）

Reading Comprehension

Directions: Please give brief answers to the following questions.

1. 请说明该备忘录的来源国与目标国。
2. 请简述该备忘录的主要内容。
3. 从格式上看，该备忘录是否符合要求？有无需要补充的地方？
4. 从内容上看，该备忘录是否完整？能否达到有效传递信息的目的？

Memorandum of Understanding Concerning Diplomatic Privileges and Immunities

I. Premises of the Liaison Office and Its Functions

1. The premises of the Liaison Office shall be inviolable. The agents of the receiving State may not enter them except with the consent of the principal officer of the Liaison Office.
2. The receiving State shall take appropriate measures to protect the premises of the Liaison Office from intrusion, damage, disturbance of the peace or impairment of its dignity.
3. The archives, documents, official correspondence and all forms of communication of the Liaison Office shall be inviolable at all times and wherever they may be.
4. The premises of the Liaison Office, its furnishings and property, shall be immune from search, requisition, attachment or execution.
5. The Liaison Office and its personnel shall be exempt from all national, regional or municipal taxes in respect of the mission, other than such as represent payment for specific services rendered.
6. The fees and charges levied by the Liaison Office in thecourse of its official duties shall be exempt from ail dues and taxes.

II. Personnel of the Liaison Office

1. The persons of personnel of the Liaison Office shall be inviolable. They

shall not be subject to any form of arrest or detention. It shall be the responsibility of the receiving State to protect such personnel from any attack on their persons, freedom or dignity.

2. Personnel of the Liaison Office shall enjoy immunity from thecriminal jurisdiction of the receiving State. They shall also enjoy immunity from its civil and administrative jurisdiction, except in respectof private immovable property held for personal, non-official use; professional or commercial activities exercised outside official functions; or an action relating to succession to property in which they are involved as a private person and not on behalf of the sending State. Personnel of the Liaison Office are not obliged to give evidence as witnesses.
3. Personnel of the Liaison Office shall be exempt from all dues and taxes, personal, real, national or municipal except those usually levied by the receiving State on the diplomatic agents of third countries in accordance with international law and custom.
4. The receiving State shall exempt the personnel of the Liaison Office from all personal or public services, and from military obligations such as those connected with requisitioning, military obligations and billeting.
5. The private residences of the personnel of the Liaison Office shall enjoy the same inviolability and protection as the premises of the mission. His property, papers and correspondence, except as provided in Section II, Paragraph 2, above, shall likewise be inviolable.
6. The members of the family of personnel of the Liaison Office forming part of the same household shall enjoy the privileges and immunities enjoyed by him with the exception of those outlined in Section IV, which may be exercised on their behalf by the personnel of the Liaison Office.
7. The private servants of personnel of the Liaison Office shall, if they are not nationals of or permanently resident in the receiving State, be exempt from dues and taxes on the emoluments they receive by reason

of their employment. They may be extended other privileges and immunities on a reciprocal basis.

8. Every person entitled to privileges and immunities shall enjoy them from the moment he enters the territory of the receiving State or, if he is already in its territory, from the moment his appointmentis notified to the receiving State. Such privileges and immunities shall continue, even in the event of armed conflict, until he leaves the territory of the receiving State.
9. In ease of the death of a member of the Liaison Office, the members of his family shall continue to enjoy the privileges and immunities to which he was entitled until the expiry of a reasonable period within which to leave the country. The movable property of the deceased and his family shall be permitted to be taken out of the country. Such property shall be exempt from taxes. This exemption shall not, however, apply to immovable property held for personal rather than Official use.
10. Without prejudice to their privileges and immunities, it is the duty of all persons enjoying such privileges and immunities to respect the laws and regulations of the receiving State.

III. Diplomatic Couriers and Pouches

Diplomatic couriers of the sending State or its Liaison Office, whether professional or ad hoc shall be protected by the receiving State in the performance of their functions. They shall enjoy personal inviolability and shall not be liable to any form of arrest or detention. The diplomatic pouch, whether accompanied or unaccompanied, shall not be opened or detained.

IV. Importation of Goods for Official or Personal Use

1. The receiving State shall grant exemption from all customs duties, taxes, and related duties other than charges for storage, cartage and similar services, on articles for the official use of the Liaison Office; and articles for the personal use of personnel of the Liaison Office or members of his family forming part of his households, including articles

intended for his establishment.

2. The personal baggage of personnel of the Liaison Office shall be exempt from inspection, unless there are serious grounds for presuming that it contains articles not covered by the exemptions mentioned in paragraph I of this Article, or articles the import or export of which is prohibited by the law or controlled by the quarantine regulations of the receiving State. Such inspection shall be conducted only in the presence of the authorized representative of the Liaison Office.

V. The present Memorandum of Understanding may be amended at any time by mutual agreement between the Governments of the People's Republic of China and the United States of America.

April 14, 1973

（文献来源：黄金祺编：《英汉对照外交文献文书教程》（上册），世界知识出版社 2004 年版，第 156 – 159 页。）

Reading Comprehension

Directions: In this part, you will have to go over the passage quickly and choose the best answer from the four choices marked A, B, C and D.

1. The premises of the Liaison Office shall be immune from the following except ________.

   A. search

   B. requisition

   C. service providing

   D. attachment and execution

2. Personnel of the Liaison Office shall enjoy immunity from ________.

   A. civil jurisdiction

   B. administrative jurisdiction

   C. destruction of public property

D. both A and B

3. The receiving State shall not grant exemption from ________ .
   A. charges for storage service
   B. taxes
   C. custom duties
   D. articles for the personal use
4. Which of following statement is true?
   A. Every person entitled to privileges and immunities shall enjoy them from the moment he enters the territory.
   B. The members of the family of personnel of the Liaison Office shall not enjoy the privileges and immunities.
   C. The persons of personnel of the Liaison Office shall be inviolable.
   D. The agents of the receiving State may not enter except with the consent of the principal officer of the Liaison Office.
5. What is the subject of the memorandum?
   A. to state diplomatic privileges and immunities.
   B. to make clear services provided for personnel of the Liaison Office.
   C. to clarify the rules of importation of goods for official or personal use.
   D. to introduce the information on protecting diplomatic couriers and pouches.

2.4 Exercises
课后练习

- **True or False**

Directions: Read the following sentences and decide whether they are true or false.

1. Letters of credence are the most formal form of exchange between states, with formal modes of address such as titles and styles being

used.

2. A letter of recall is the negative signal for the bilateral relations.
3. A letter of recall can be used as a means of diplomatic protest.
4. The Note is the most commonly used form of written communication in diplomatic intercourse.
5. A Verbal Note is also a form of written communication and an oral one as the term "Verbal" might indicate.
6. With the trend of simplifying formalities in diplomatic practice, a Formal Note can now be used on many occasions which would otherwise require a Verbal Note.
7. Essentially, Memorandum differs from a Note.
8. A Memorandum is prepared either before or after an interview as a formal record of the oral communication or conversation.
9. A Memorandum can never be presented personally following an interview.

- **Gap-filling**

Directions: Complete each sentence with appropriate words.

1. Until a head of state or his or her delegate formally accepts a letter of credence, an/a ________ does not formally assume ________, including the possession of ________.
2. (A Formal Note) It deals with ________ more important political affairs or diplomatic formalities. A Formal Note is drafted in the ________ person. A Formal Note, as mentioned, is used to deal with comparatively more important affairs and diplomatic ________.
3. The kind of paper used in each case will depend upon the ________ of the Memorandum concerned. For a Chinese Memorandum, the traditional ________ is used. In the case of an important Memorandum, the paper bearing our ________ is recommended.

• Multiple Choices

Directions: In this part there are 7 incomplete sentences. For each sentence there are four choices marked A, B, C and D. Choose the ONE answer that best completes the sentence.

1. When two countries maintain relations at the chargé level, the letter of credence will be written by the ________ of the sending state, and addressed to the foreign minister of the receiving state.

   A. foreign minister　　B. head of state
   C. prime minister　　D. Ministry of Foreign Affairs

2. A letter of credence is a formal letter usually sent by one head of state to another head of state that formally grants ________ to a named individual (usually but not always a diplomat) to be the sending country's ambassador in the receiving country.

   A. diplomatic accreditation　　B. diplomatic immunity
   C. help　　D. trust

3. Letters of credence are presented personally to the receiving head of state by ________ in a formal ceremony.

   A. ambassador-designates　　B. diplomat
   C. ambassador/consul　　D. head of state

4. A Formal Note is essentially a formal personal letter. It is the most formal form of ________ used between the foreign minister of one country and his counterpart in another, between a foreign minister and a head of mission or between one head of mission and another.

   A. written communication　　B. communication
   C. changing information　　D. making a decision

5. It is a ________ person Note used between diplomatic services of different counties, for instance, between one ministry of foreign affairs and another, between a ministry of foreign affairs and embassy, between one embassy and another, and so on.

   A. first

B. second

C. third

D. first, second and third are all OK

6. With a view to ________, a Memorandum is prepared either before or after an interview as a formal record of the oral communication or conversation.

   A. being polite B. avoiding misunderstanding

   C. leaving a positive impression D. convenience

7. All of the following information can be included in a Memorandum except ________ .

   A. a detailed statement of facts

   B. thorough expression of views

   C. an elaborate argument on certain issues

   D. private information

• Translation

Directions: translate the following sentences into the target language.

English-Chinese Translation

1. Being desirous to maintain, without interruption, the relations of friendship and good understanding so happily subsisting between Pakistan and the People's Republic of China, we have made choices of our Trusty and well-beloved Mr. × × to reside with You in the character of Our Ambassador Extraordinary and Plenipotentiary for Pakistan.
2. I request your Excellency to receive him favourably and give full credence to all of that he may represent to your Excellency in the name of the Government of the People's Republic of China.
3. We request that you will give entire credence to all that Mr. × × shall communicate to you in our name, more especially when he shall renew

to you the assurances of the lively interest which we take in everything that affects the welfare and prosperity of the People's Republic of China.

4. Despite this clear knowledge of the boundary, the Chinese forces have, during the last month, while notes were being exchanged for holding talks and discussions, intruded into Indian territory in the eastern sector and have been attacking Indian forces since 20th September.
5. It is obviously the Chinese practice to alter the status quo unilaterally whenever they can.
6. The Central People's Governmentare fully aware of the views of the Government of India on the adjustment of Sino-Tibetan relations.
7. The Central People's Government must be aware that opinion in the United Nations has been steadily veering round to the admission of China into that organization before the close of the present session.

Chinese-English Translation

1. 为了建立和发展中华人民共和国与美利坚合众国之间的友好合作关系，我根据中华人民共和国全国人民代表大会常务委员会的决定，任命××先生为中华人民共和国驻美利坚合众国的特命全权大使。

2. 该大使的品质与才能足以完全保证他必能尽他的全力，完成他所担负的崇高使命以获得阁下的信赖。

3. 本人具此信心，谨请阁下对该大使惠予接待，并对该大使以本人名义向阁下所陈述之一切，予以完全信任。谨祝阁下政躬康泰，贵国国运昌隆。

4. 双方各自后撤二十公里的建议，显然有碍于印度方面不仅在西段和中段，而且在东段进行这种侵略活动。

5. 中国政府准备在十月十五日接待印度方面派出的代表。中国政府并建议立即通过外交途径商定其他有关细节。

6. 中国政府对于历届旧政府的外债，一概不予承认，也不承担偿还的义务。这是我国政府的一贯立场。

7. 中国政府一贯主张在和平共处五项原则的基础上发展中美两国的关系。

• Simulative Exercise

Suppose China is going to establish an embassy in A city of B country, please write a Note to inform another embassy of the establishment of it and the designation of its Chargé d'affairs.

3 Documents for Social Occasions
第三章 社交文书

Abstract

Document for social occasions is a type of document widely used as an important form of diplomatic correspondence. Formal letters can be exchanged between national leaders, between diplomats of higher ranks, and between foreign ministers, etc. They can be used for dealing with important political affairs, putting forward proposals, invitations, personal greetings, offering congratulations or condolences and so on.

Two types of documents will be introduced in terms of their definition, functions and contents, in order to understand the various application areas and objectives. The selected bilingual case studies aim to enhance the understanding of the two documents and to promote the writing skills through practices.

内容概览

社交文书是我们在外事交往活动中所使用的文书种类，具有往来性、灵活性和礼节性等特点。社交文书多数情况下都是在相互之间进行的。一方发给另一方一份邀请函，另一方一般都要给对方复电或复函。其灵活性主要体现在写作风格上。这种文书写起来比较简便，很灵活。虽说其写作格式不死板，但仍有大体固定的行文方式。此外，撰写社交文书还要注意向对方问候和致意等国际交往礼节。例如，在称呼方面，要尽量尊重对方，特别是对国家首脑、政府要员等，要按照国际惯例写尊称。

本章详细介绍邀请函与贺电两种外交函件的定义、作用和内容，明确其使用场合及目的。本章以精选的双语案例作为范本，从正反两方面加强读者对两种文书的理解，并通过实战演练提高相关人员关于这两种文书的写作水平。

3.1 Letter of Invitation
第一节 邀请函

Basic Knowledge
一、基础知识

Introduction

A Letter of Invitation, or Invitation Letter, is a document that presents a formal request for the presence of an individual, a group of people or an organization at an event. An invitation letter may be formal or informal. It could be printed on paper or sent via email.

Invitation letters can be used for a variety of events such as weddings, graduation ceremonies, annual dinners, anniversary parties and birthday parties. They could also be used to invite guest speakers, keynote speakers and workshop facilitators to special meetings and events.

（一）简介

邀请函又称邀请信，是单位或个人在举办诸如访问、学术研讨、产品展销等重要活动前，请相关领导人、专家、学者和其他知名人士前来参加的信函。邀请函在外事活动中使用频率很高，是重要的外交文体。

Contents and Features

An invitation letter usually contains some information about the host, the date and the time of the event, the venue of the event and how to accept the invitation. Invitations are usually sent many days in advance of the event, to give the invitees time to respond to the invitation.

Invitation letters to events can be divided into two groups-Invitation Letters to individuals for a special role in an event and Invitation Letters to individuals to attend an event.

(二) 内容和特点

按用途分类，可分为会议邀请函（专为庆祝会、纪念会、座谈会等发出）；活动类邀请函（专为仪式、宴请等发出）；工作事务类邀请函（专为事务的洽谈与合作等发出）。

邀请函除了具备社交文书的共同特点外，还具有以下特点：

1. 内容精简。邀请对象、原因、时间、地点及相关事项等一目了然，力求篇幅简短。

2. 措辞典雅。语言庄重、典雅，敬语谦辞合乎情景。

3. 外观精美。注重外观形式的美观和精致，版面设计根据活动的内容和风格力求新颖别致。

（李薇，2014）

Writing Requirement

The professional invitation letter should be written in a formal tone.

The introduction allows the host and sender to introduce themselves, as well as the organization in which they have chosen to represent. A simple background of the individual or company will suffice.

Next, in the body of the letter it is important to outline all of the information about the event. The date and time should be included as well as the theme and purpose for the event. At this point, a date by which guests should provide their reply should be mentioned, and it may also contain any information regarding special roles played at the event, attire and items required for the guest to bring.

Then, the appreciation for the guest to attend the party should be shown. This can be completed with a formal note, stating that you look forward to seeing the individual at the event. Remember, this needs to keep in tone with the rest of the letter.

The conclusion should contain the sign off and a line that ties the complete letter together, drawing the end of the invitation, with a salutation and a signature.

（三）写作要求

邀请函主要由标题、称谓、正文及落款四部分组成。

1. 标题。标题可由“事由 + 文种”组成，或“会议名称 + 文种”组成。

2. 称谓。在开头顶格书写被邀请者的姓名或单位名称。个人姓名后应加职务、职称或“阁下”“同志”“先生”“女士”等相应的称谓。

3. 正文。正文应包含开头问候语、主体和信末问候语等内容。

4. 落款。署上邀请者的姓名（单位）和日期。

（谢世洋，2014）

Case Studies
二、案例分析

案例一

Place, date

Your Excellency,

On behalf of the Government and people of the People's Republic of China, I have the honour to extend to you an invitation to pay a visit to our country with your party. I earnestly hope that it will be convenient for you to provide the President, the Premier, the Government and the People of our country an opportunity of having you in their midst.

I can assure you that a visit to China by a person of Your Excellency's eminence would lead to a further promotion and strengthening of the cordial and happy relations that exist between China and …

It would be convenient if I was allowed to convey your wishes in the matter to our Government at an early date in order to finalize the arrangements for the visit.

I avail myself of this opportunity to renew to Your Excellency the assurances of my highest consideration.

(signed)

Ambassador of the People's Republic of China to ________

His Excellency ________,

Prime Minister of ________,

PLACE

His Excellency,

President of,

(Signed)

President of the People's
Republic of China

(文献来源：黄金祺编：《英汉对照外交文献文书教程》（上册），世界知识出版社2004年版，第198－199页。)

Analysis

The Letter of Invitation consists of appellation, body and signature, without title. It is designed mainly for those invitees to pay a visit in China and also expresses the good wishes for diplomatic staff's successful visit and meaningful stay in China.

案例二

环保座谈会邀请函

尊敬的威尔逊：

瑞典对华投资环境保护考察团今日将来我市考察。拟于三月十日上午九点，在长城饭店外宾接待室召开一个小型环保专家座谈会，您是美国著名的环保学专家，请届时莅临座谈会。

此致

春安

××市外事办公室

一九九八年三月一日

（公章）

（文献来源：李德芳等主编：《应用文写作》，北京师范大学出版社 1999 年版，第 171 页。）

分析概要

这份邀请函由标题、称谓、正文和落款几部分组成。在简要介绍相关背景后，清楚标明座谈会的时间和地点，表达了对受邀人参会的希望，措辞应得体、委婉、礼貌。

Supplementary Readings

三、拓展阅读

December 10, 2008

Dear Mrs. Coling:

My name is Susan Harris and I am writing on behalf of the students at Lockwood Middle School.

A significant amount of the students at the school have been working on a project which relates to the unemployment problem within the youth demographic of Lockwood. You are invited to attend a presentation that will be held within the media room of the school where a variety of proposals that will demonstrate the ability of the community to develop employment opportunities for the youth within the community.

At the presentation, there will be several students receiving awards which will recognize them within the community from the Mayor. Refreshments will also be available at the presentation.

As one of the prominent figures in the community, we would be honored by your attendance. Our special presentation will be held at our school auditorium on January 16th. Please reply by Monday the 9th of January to confirm your attendance to the function.

We look forward to seeing you there, Sincerely,

Signature

Ms. Susan Harris

Reading Comprehension

Directions: Please give brief answers to the following questions.

1. Can you generalize some basic features of the above Letter of Invitation?
2. Are there, if any, deficiencies in both content and structure of the above Letter of Invitation?
3. What is your idea to improve the above Letter of Invitation?

×××劳动党中央委员会第一书记××同志

×××人民议会主席团主席××同志

×××部长会议主席××同志

亲爱的同志们：

××××年十月一日是中华人民共和国成立的第×周年国庆。中国共产党中央委员会和中华人民共和国政府热诚地邀请×××派遣党政代表团前来参加中华人民共和国第×周年国庆典礼。

我们恳切地渴望×××接受我们这一邀请，并且希望早日得到关于××党政代表团成员的通知。

中国共产党中央委员会主席×××（签字）

中华人民共和国主席×××（签字）

中华人民共和国全国人民代表大会常务委员会委员长×××（签字）

中华人民共和国国务院总理×××（签字）

××××年×月×日于北京

（文献来源：黄金祺编：《英汉对照外交文献文书教程》（上册），世界知识出版社2004年版，第196页。）

Reading Comprehension

Directions: Please give brief answers to the following questions.

1. 请说明该邀请函的来源国与目标国。
2. 请简述该邀请函的主要内容。
3. 从格式上看，该邀请函是否符合要求？有无需要补充的地方？
4. 从内容上看，该邀请函是否完整？能否达到有效传递信息的目的？

3.2 Congratulatory Telegram

第二节 贺电

Basic Knowledge

一、基础知识

Introduction

A congratulatory telegram, or congratulation letter, is used in both personal and business situations. Its primary purpose is to formally congratulate a person or an organization for an outstanding achievement. With a congratulation letter, we can show others their efforts in achieving their goals and also make them proud of their achievements. Congratulation letters can be sent directly to the recipient and also be published or broadcast to the public. When writing it, always keep it in mind that to keep the tone of the letter pleasant.

（一）简介

贺电是领导机关、单位或领导人以个人名义发给有关单位、集体、个人，以表示祝贺、赞颂的电报。贺电的内容十分广泛，可以祝贺国家领导人任职，可以祝贺国家重大会议或重要纪念日；也可以祝贺对方取得优异的成绩等。重要的贺电往往对广大群众有很大的鼓舞和教育作用。

Contents and Features

A congratulation letter usually includes the heading, title, body, ending and signature. First, make clear about the purpose of writing the letter. Second, state the exact achievement you are referencing, along with indicating the source of the good news.

A congratulation message should extend the cordial greetings and indicate the significance of the achievement. Keep the message simple by limiting the letter to one page.

Be sincere in writing a congratulation letter. Keep it positive, simple, and straight to the point.

（二）内容与特点

贺电行文有鲜明的特点：

1. 祝福要真诚

祝贺词作为加强联系，增进双方交流的一种重要手段，所表示的感情要热烈真挚，发自内心，给人以温暖和鼓舞的力量。内容言之有情，言之有物。

2. 定位要准确

写作时要注意彼此关系，符合双方身份。对双方的身份和地位的差异、关系的深浅、往来的亲疏，都要有清醒的认识，这样才能做到中心突出，措辞得体，礼貌周到。

3. 评价要恰当

内容要实事求是，评价成绩、颂扬和祝贺要恰如其分。表示决心要切实可行，不可言过其实，空喊口号。

4. 篇幅要精短

语言要简短生动、流畅得体，长而空是不受欢迎的。可恰当地使用对偶、比喻等修辞手法，使贺电显得优美文雅，但不能堆砌华丽的辞藻。书面表达和口头表达均需如此。

（张浩，2014）

Writing Requirement

The congratulatory telegram should express praise and approval of the reader's accomplishment. It should be simple and concise. Keep it positive and don't include any negative comments. Do not exaggerate your congratulatory words or your letter would seem to be sarcastic or mocking. Besides, a telegram of congratulation should be sent immediately, in order to convey the timely compliment.

（三）写作要求

1. 标题。正中写“贺电”两个字，另起一行顶格写被祝贺单位或个人的称呼。若是写给个人的，要加“先生”或相应的称呼。

2. 正文。简述对方所取得成绩的社会背景或重要会议召开的历史条件。简要说明对方在哪些方面取得了成绩，表示热烈的祝贺与称赞。

3. 结尾。写上表示祝愿的话，如“祝大会圆满成功”“祝您健康长寿”等。

4. 署名。

（张浩，2014）

Case Studies
二、案例分析

案例一

Conference of African Heads of State,
ADDIS ABABA

On the occasion of the opening of the Conference of African Heads of State, I have the honour, on behalf of the Government of the People's Republic of China and the Chinese people and in my own name, to send greetings to the Conference. May the Conference make new contributions towards the promotion of friendship and cooperation among African countries, towards the African people's struggle to oppose old and new colonialism and to win or safeguard their national independence, and towards the strengthening of Asian-African solidarity and the defense of worldpeace. I wish the Conference every success.

Chou En-lai,
Premier of the State Council
of the People's Republic of China
Peking, May 21, 1963

（文献来源：黄金祺编:《英汉对照外交文献文书教程》（上册），世界知识出版社2004年版，第293－294页。）

Analysis

In terms of structure, the congratulatory telegram consists of addressing, body, conclusion and signature. It was addressed to celebrate the international conference of African state leaders. The body part mainly deals with the warm congratulations and best wishes from the People's Republic of China, with the conclusion expressing the wishes for a successful conference. The final part of the telegram is signature.

分析概要

就结构而言，这份贺电包括了四个部分：称呼、正文、结尾、落款。称呼部分点明了祝贺的对象，并使用了恰当的称谓。其后是正式祝贺对方就任总统并表达良好祝愿。结尾是对两国未来关系的展望，最后是落款及日期。

Supplementary Readings
三、拓展阅读

请仔细阅读以下内容，回答问题。

Conference of Heads of State or Government
of Non-aligned Countries,
NEW DELHI,

On the occasion of the convocation of the Seventh Conference of Heads of State or Government of Non-aligned Countries, I would like to extend, on behalf of the Chinese Government and people, our warm congratulations.

Tremendous changes have taken place in international situation since the First Summit Conference of the Non-aligned Countries. Together with the peoples of other countries, the peoples of the non-aligned countries have won significant victories in their struggles against imperialism, colonialism and neo-colonialism, racism, and all forms of foreign aggression, occupation, control, interference and hegemony. The non-aligned movement has become a political force exerting important influence on the present international arena.

The Chinese Government and people deeply appreciate the purposes of the non-aligned movement and its independent, sovereign and non-bloc principles, highly appraise the positive role played by the non-aligned movement in international affairs, firmly support the non-aligned countries in their struggle to safeguard national independence, develop national economy, maintain international security and establish a new international economic order.

May the non-aligned movement continue to adhere to its lofty purposes and principles and make new contributions to enhanced solidarity and cooperation, to the struggle against imperialism, colonialism, foreign occupation and domination and hegemony, and to the great cause of world peace and humanprogress.

Beijing, 6 March 1983

（文献来源：黄金祺编：《英汉对照外交文献文书教程》（上册），世界知识出版社 2004 年版，第 294－295 页。）

Reading Comprehension

Directions: In this part, you will have to go over the passage quickly and choose the best answer from the four choices marked A, B, C and D.

1. This congratulatory telegram is addressed to ________.
   A. the opening of international conference
   B. the inauguration of a foreign state leader
   C. the celebration of a state leader's birthday
   D. None of the above
2. In term of the structure, which part is missing in this congratulatory telegram?
   A. appellation

B. body
C. conclusion
D. signature

3. Which of the following is not true?
   A. The background information is presented right after the congratulations.
   B. The best wishes are expressed in the conclusion.
   C. The appellation is incomplete.
   D. The theme of the telegram is clear.

3.3 Exercises
课后练习

- **True or False**

Directions: Read the following sentences and decide whether they are true or false.

1. An invitation letter should only be written to invite states for a friendly visit.
2. The format of the letter depends on the nature of the occasion and the person you are inviting.
3. Letter of invitation should not be in the first person.
4. Invitation cards would involve complete names instead of abbreviations.
5. Invitation cards should be written in first person.
6. An invitation card has no abbreviations or contractions expect for name titles.
7. A congratulatory telegram should put the address and the date of the letter before the body.
8. A congratulatory telegram could sometimes convey negative or selfish feelings.

9. A congratulatory telegram should be simple and concise.

• Gap-filling

Directions: Complete each sentence with appropriate words.

1. An invitation letter may be ________ or ________. It could be printed on paper or sent via ________.
2. Invitation letters can be used for a variety of events such as weddings, ________, annual dinners, anniversary parties and ________.
3. A congratulatory telegram should praise the ________, also discuss the significance of it, keep it ________ and don't include ________ or ________.

• Multiple Choices

Directions: In this part there are 5 incomplete sentences. For each sentence there are four choices marked A, B, C and D. Choose the ONE answer that best completes the sentence.

1. Document for social occasions is a type of document widely used as an important form of ________.

   A. diplomatic correspondence   B. government policies
   C. referential documents   D. none of the above

2. Documents for social occasionscan be used for ________.

   A. putting forward proposals   B. offering condolences
   C. dealing with political affairs   D. all of above

3. The professional invitation letter should be written in a ________ tone.

   A. informal   B. formal
   C. casual   D. serious

4. Acongratulatory letter may not include ________.

   A. address   B. body
   C. title   D. signature

5. Which of the following is not correct regarding congratulatory letter?
   A. It should be simple and concise.
   B. It should be sent immediately.
   C. It should express praise and approval of the reader's accomplishment.
   D. You canexaggerate your congratulatory words.

• Translation

Directions: translate the following sentences into the target language.

English-Chinese Translation

1. On behalf of the Government and people of the People's Republic of China and in my own name, I have the honour to invite Your Excellency to China for a friendly visit at a date convenient to Your Excellency.
2. I am sure that Your Excellency's visit will not only make fresh contributions to the furtherance of the friendship between our two countries.
3. As for the specific date and programme of the visit, I will respect Your Excellency's wishes in arranging them.
4. Our cooperations have taken many positive forms, but agriculture and trade related exchanges seem to be the foundation in which our relationship has prospered.
5. He would be happy to arrange an itinerary to meet your interests and I can assure you that you would have very productive and memorable day in Iowa.
6. On the occasion of the United Nations Fourth World Conference On Women in Beijing, the Government of the People's Republic of China requests the pleasure of your company at welcoming ceremony at 10:00 a. m. on Monday.

7. On the occasion of the National Day of the Republic of Chile, we, on behalf of the Chinese Government and people, wish to extend warm congratulations to Your Excellency and, through Your Excellency, to the Chilean Government and people.
8. May the relations between our two countries continuously develop in the common struggle of opposing hegemonism and promoting world peace.

Chinese-English translation

1. 两国之间的友好关系和经济、文化往来在和平共处五项原则的基础上得到了顺利的发展。

2. 我们相信，中国人民和智利人民之间的深厚友谊在反对霸权主义和促进世界和平的事业中将会日益发展。

3. 正如您所知道的，爱荷华州同中国有着传统的友谊。

4. 我荣幸地代表中华人民共和国政府，并以我个人的名义邀请阁下在方便的时候来我国进行友好访问。

5. 我们开展了多种形式的合作，尤其是在农业和贸易方面，我们的关系得到长足发展。

• Simulative Exercise

Suppose India is going to celebratethe National Day. Please write a congratulatory telegram to India on behalf of the Chinese Government and people.

4 Documents for Speeches

第四章 讲演文书

Abstract

In contemporary diplomatic practice there are ample platforms for statesmen and diplomats: The United Nations, various international conferences, different occasions during an official visit (ceremony at the airport, banquets, gatherings, even a session of the legislature of the host country) and so on. Speech documents are oral statements made by state leaders or diplomats of higher rank on official or social occasions; their significance depends mainly on the importance of their substance, the occasion and the speaker. Many speeches have become historic international documents.

A diplomatic speech has no rigid forms, although there are still some general rules to follow in drafting it. Besides, like diplomacy itself, to draft a speech is an art of skill. The selected bilingual case studies aim to enhance the understanding of the speech documents and to promote the writing skills through practices.

内容概览

在当代外交实践中，政治家和外交家们有着众多的讲坛：联合国、各种国际会议、正式访问时的各种场合（机场欢迎仪式、宴会、集会，以至东道主立法机构专门安排的会议）等。讲演文书是国家领导人或高级外交官在官方或社交活动中所做的口头讲话，其重要性主要决定于它们的实质内容、场合和讲话人。

讲演文书没有严格的格式，但在起草时仍有一般规则可循。此外，像外交本身一样，起草讲演文书也是一种富含技巧的艺术。本章以精选的双语案例为范本，从正反两方面加强读者对讲演文书的理解，并通过实战演练提高相关人员关于此类文书的写作水平。

4.1 Welcoming Speech and Seeing-off Speech
第一节 欢迎词和欢送词

Basic Knowledge
一、基础知识

Introduction

In the formal occasion of the foreign affairs, the host country should play host to the foreign guests to make them feel at home, and the speech to show hospitality made by the host is called welcoming speech. When the guests are about to leave, the host will invite the guests to attend a farewell banquet. On this occasion, the host will address the guests a speech to show the clinging feelings and to strengthen their friendship, which is called seeing-off speech.

（一）简介

在外事活动的正式场合中，接待或招待客人，主人需要发表热情友好的讲话，以表示欢迎，使人感到“宾至如归”，这种讲话就是欢迎词。当客人逗留了一落时间，要离别时，主人和客人欢聚一堂，互相问候，并致祝愿，表达依依不舍之情，以增进友谊。在这种场合，主人的讲话被称为欢送词，而此时客人的回复被称为告别词。

（于云、王力，1990）

Contents and Features

There will usually be some warmly words at the beginning of the welcoming speech. In the body part of the speech, the speaker usually introduces some reasons of the guests' coming and recall what they both gained during the past cooperation and friendly contact and then put forward the tasks that they both will fulfill. Last but not least, sincere wishes are shown to the guests. Seeing-off speech is to address when the guests are leaving. It is similar to welcoming speech in content, attaching much importance to strengthening the future relations.

（二）内容和特点

欢迎词一般先在开头对宾客的来临表示热烈的欢迎；后于主体部分说明宾客来临的背景，回顾双方友好交往、愉快合作已取得的成果，并说明这些成果的意义，然后说明面临的任务，表示完成任务、增进交往、加强合作的信心。最后，用简短的语句向宾客表示良好的祝愿：祝宾客愉快，祝宾客成功，或祝宾客健康。欢送词是在欢送宾客或会议结束时发表的文辞。内容与欢迎词大致无差，重在表达主人对宾客的离去表示热烈欢送。

欢迎词和欢送词的特点大致如下:

1. 一般的欢迎词都是一种礼节性的外交或公关辞令，遣词造句十分讲究礼貌，称呼使用尊称，表达致辞者热情和友好的情感。欢迎词语言生动简洁、大方得体。

2. 欢迎词一般都比较简短，言简意赅，短小精悍，旨在进一步增强双方的交流与合作，营造和强化友好和谐的社交气氛。

3. 欢送词的特点与欢迎词的特点基本相同，口语性也是欢送词的一个显著特点之一。因此，遣词造句也应注意使用生活化的语言，使送别既富有情趣，又自然得体。

4. 欢送词还具有惜别性，表达出亲朋好友远行时的感受，表达出真切的送别之情与祝愿，格调不必过于低沉、悲伤，应把握好分别时所用言辞的分寸。

（任焕琴、吴少伟、刘莉芳，2012）

Writing Requirements

Generally, the writing of welcoming speech and seeing-off speech includes such parts as title, address, body and signature.

1. Title

Put the title in the middle of the first line. However, when addressing the public the speaker need not read the title of the speech additionally.

2. Address

The guests are always called "Ladies and gentlemen". To make it better, add "Dear" or "Honorable" before the address.

3. Body

This part is considered the most important part of the speech and should be complete and overall.

4. Signature

This part always appears in written form, but will not be read out in the public.

（三）写作要求

根据客人（单位或个人）与写作方之间存在的相互关系（或上下级，或平级不相隶属）以及欢迎或欢送的具体时空场合，准确定位欢迎或欢送时的交际立场，在措辞中注意表现出恰如其分的情感浓烈程度。内容上侧重于双方交往的积极方面，具有很强的礼仪性。一般不在此讨论双方的分歧和重大差异。

欢迎词和欢送词都是在特定场合当众宣读的，因此语句要准确，不能出现有歧义的字词，遣词造句应当晓畅通俗，符合生活中口语的使用规范。该类文辞篇幅不宜过长，避免套话、空话，除特殊场合外，一般控制在3—5分钟。

具体来说，欢迎词或欢送词主要分为以下几部分：

1. 标题

第一行居中写上“欢迎词”或“欢送词”，也可在之前加上具体的场合，还可在场合之前加上致辞人的名字，如“××在×××上的欢送词”，正式的场合或报刊刊登常用后两种形式。欢迎词和欢送词一般都是当众宣读内容，并不直接宣读标题。

2. 称谓

统称“女士们、先生们”“各位来宾”等，也可在之前加上“尊敬的”“敬爱的”“亲爱的”等前缀。

3. 正文

欢迎词的正文通常包括这样几个层次的内容：首先要对对方的到来表示热烈的欢迎，并点明自己和对方的身份，如“我谨代表……向……表示热烈的欢迎”；随后可概要介绍有关自己所在区域或行业方面的情况；接着写明对方来访的目的和意义，或简单回顾双方交往的历史，并表明愿意继续合作的意愿；最后，再次对对方的光临表示欢迎，并预祝对方的来访能够取得圆满成功。

欢送词的正文结构和欢迎词的大体相同。首先，对对方即将离去表示欢送和不舍之情；接着对对方的来访表示充分的肯定，并表达加强交往的期待；最后在结尾处再次表示欢送。

4. 落款

在正文右下方写上致辞的机关、人名和日期。如果在标题中已经表明，此处可以略去。

（粟斌，2012）

Case Studies
二、案例分析

案例一

Remarks in an Exchange of Toasts at State Dinner
by Barack Obama, President of the United States of America
State Dining Room, White House, Washington
January 19, 2011

Good evening, everybody. Please have a seat. On behalf of Michelle and myself, welcome to the White House. And thank you for joining us as we host President Hu and the Chinese delegation, and as we pay tribute to the bonds between two great nations and two proud peoples.

There are too many distinguished guests to mention all of you tonight. But I do want to acknowledge a few who have championed relations between our nations: First of all, President Jimmy Carter and his wonderful wife Rosalyn Carter are here. As well as President Bill Clinton and my outstanding Secretary of State, Hillary Clinton.

President Hu, we have met today in a spirit of mutual respect: the United States-the oldest democracy in the world, and China-one of the oldest civilizations in the world. And while it's easy to focus on our differences of culture and perspective, let us never forget the values that our people share: a reverence for family; the belief that, with education and hard work and with sacrifice, the future is what we make it; and most of all, the desire to give our children a better life.

Let's also never forget that throughout our history our people have worked together for mutual progress. We've traded together for more than 200 years. We stood together in the Second World War. Chinese immigrants and Chinese Americans have helped to build America, including many who join us here tonight.

The Chinese and American people work together and create new opportunities together every single day. Mr. President, today we've shown that our governments can work together as well, for our mutual benefit. And that includes this bit of news-under a new agreement, our National Zoo will continue to dazzle children and visitors with the beloved giant pandas.

I'm told that there is a Chinese proverb that says: If you want one year of prosperity, then grow grain. If you want 10 years of prosperity, then grow trees. But if you want 100 years of prosperity, then you grow people.

And so I propose a toast-to our people, the citizens of the People's Republic of China and the United States of America. May they grow together in friendship. May they prosper together in peace. And may they realize their dream of the future for themselves, for their children, and for their grandchildren.

Ganbei.

（文献来源：https: //www. whitehouse. gov/the-press-office/2011/01/19/remarks-president-obama-and-president-hu-peoples-republic-china-exchange，检索日期：2015 年 11 月 3 日。）

Analysis

In terms of structure, the welcoming speech consists of title, address and body. Since welcoming speech is usually announced improvisionally, it always goes without mentioning the signature. Meanwhile, it should be noticed that this speech carries some sense of proposing toasts.

案例二

西哈努克亲王在机场送别刘少奇主席时的讲话
（一九六三年五月六日）

共和国主席先生和夫人，

中华人民共和国尊敬的客人和亲爱的朋友们，

刘少奇主席阁下、王光美女士和我们的中国老朋友们过一会儿就要离开我们了。我们一起度过了几天愉快的日子。他们给我们留下了美好的印象，同时还给我们留下了一件无限宝贵、坚如磐石的东西：两国人民和两国之间的友好和团结。刘少奇主席阁下的访问是圆满成功的。这一个全面的成功对我们共同的未来肯定具有重大的意义，因为它向全世界证实了三个月以前我们在北京所说的话：柬埔寨和中国决心携手前进，世界上没有任何力量能够阻挡它们。

昨天，我们在联合声明上签了字，它表明我们观点的一致，并重申我们的团结。在我们两国的合作中，我们将取得对命运的更大的信心，并确定我们将能胜利地抗拒帝国主义的各种诡计。

请允许我表达我们对世界上最伟大强盛的国家之一的元首光临我们小国的激动心情，这在我国历史上至今还是独一无二的。贵宾们十分宽宏大量地向我们说，我们的欢迎在各方面都是配得上他们对我们的尊敬的。我们的条件是微小的，但是我们对他们与中华人民共和国的感激和热爱是巨大的。他们对我们的进步——这些进步和他们的进步比较起来是极为微小的——和我们的牺牲的评价，是对我们继续进行国家建设的最大鼓舞。

我建议以王后陛下、政府、柬埔寨人民以及我个人的名义，请共和国主席先生转达我们对英勇的中国人民及其领导者们最热忱的祝愿，祝他们幸福，祝他们在新的跃进中成功，祝中华人民共和国强盛；并请你告诉他们可以相信柬埔寨及其人民的兄弟友谊和团结。

中华人民共和国万岁！

伟大的中国人民万岁！

柬中两国牢不可破的友谊和团结万岁！

（文献来源：《和平外交和睦邻政策的典范——刘少奇主席访问印度尼西亚、缅甸、柬埔寨、越南》，人民出版社 1963 年版，第 71－72 页。）

分析概要

这篇欢送词是1963年西哈努克亲王在机场送别刘少奇主席时的讲话。在正文中，西哈努克亲王回顾了与刘少奇主席及夫人度过的愉快时光以及中柬双方共同取得的成果。最后，表达真挚的祝愿和欢送。

Supplementary Readings

三、拓展阅读

请仔细阅读以下两则欢迎词的内容，回答问题。

佩里先生：

在复活节即将到来的时候，我代表我们××公司，并以我个人的名义，向您和您的代表团一行人的光临表示最热烈的欢迎并致以良好的祝愿和问候。

我们非常高兴地看到过去一年中我们之间的合作是多么令人愉快，也衷心地希望我们之间的业务关系在未来的岁月将继续下去。

在我欣悉您已经被任命为×××××电气公司董事会董事之际，请接受我最良好的祝愿。

（文献来源：邱宣煌：《财经应用文写作训练》，东北财经大学出版社2001年版，第128页。）

Reading Comprehension

Directions: Please give brief answers to the following questions.

1. 请简述以上欢迎词的主要内容。
2. 思考该欢迎词在措辞上是否有不妥，若有，请指出并改正。
3. 从内容上看，该欢迎词是否全面，是否已起到欢迎词应有的作用？

4. 从形式上看，该欢迎词是否完整，若不完整，请补充改正。

泰国渔业局局长 Somying Piumsombun 女士的欢迎词

Excellency, Theera Wongsamut, Minister of Agriculture and Cooperatives of Thailand, Mr Kevern Cochrane. Director of the Fisheries and Aquaculture Resources Use and Conservation Division of FAO, Distinguished Delegates, Ladies and Gentlemen, on behalf of the Department of Fisheries, I wish to extend our warm welcome to FAO colleagues and all delegates from more than 50 countries for their participation in the Fifth Session of the COFI Sub-Committee on Aquaculture held this week in beautiful Phuket. I would also like to express our sincere thanks to FAO for the close collaboration that made this meeting possible today.

Fisheries and aquaculture plays a vital role not only to rural development but also to the global and national economy in particular its contribution to food security. Thailand, as one member of FAO, has been very committed to the sustainable practices of fisheries and aquaculture for many decades. In fact, this year the Department of Fisheries has reached its 84th year of national service. Through the eight decades of experiences and development, our Department has contributed toward various activities including capture fisheries, aquaculture, post-harvest technology, fisheries conservation, fisheries technology transfer, high sea fisheries and international fisheries affairs. In 2008, fisheries and aquaculture contributed about 3. 2 million metric tonnes, of which 42 percent came from aquaculture. As for aquaculture, Thailand has extensive experience in marine shrimp culture which led us to significant success during the past three decades. Last year, we exported 1. 9 million metric tonnes of fishery products valuing USD 6. 5 billion. Of that figure, nearly four hundred thousand tonnes of shrimp were exported amounting to USD 2. 6 billion.

Thailand as an ASEAN member country, which contributes 20 percent of global fisheries and aquaculture production, has worked hand in hand with the other nine countries to strengthen our fisheries and aquaculture in the region. The close collaboration with various regional and international organizations such as FAO SEAFDEC, NACA, World Fish Center, INFOFISH etc. has enabled us to strengthen our cooperation for the improvement of fisheries and aquaculture development in the region.

We appreciate the kind support from FAO in continuously developing technical guidelines on aquaculture certification since the request of the third session of the Sub-Committee on Aquaculture in India. The guidelines have been a long process through a global review of six expert workshops, the fourth session of the Sub-Committee on Aquaculture in Chile and the latest technical consultation at FAO headquarters early this year. We look forward to see the technical guidelines on aquaculture certification endorsed by the fifth session of the Sub-Committee so that they can be implemented globally both for public and private sectors. We all hope that the success in the implementation of these guidelines will minimize the confusion among the different certification schemes worldwide.

Whilst the technical guidelines on aquaculture certification were under process, ASEAN joined hands through the mechanism of ASEAN Shrimp Alliance using the principles of the guidelines as a basis to develop ASEAN Shrimp GAP. In fact, both ASEAN Shrimp GAP and its Development Strategy have just been endorsed, in principle, by the ASEAN Sectoral Working Group on Fisheries 1st June.

Ladies and Gentlemen,

The meeting agenda includes a three day discussion with various important matters. On Thursday, as a break for the Sub-Committee Members, we have provided a series of study trips combined with a technical and leisure tour. Towards the end of the tour, as promised in Chile, we will invite all delegates to a party by the beautiful Phuket beach where they will enjoy a variety of Thai quality seafood selections. For today's reception we are pleased to invite you to enjoy our welcome dinner at the Phuket Fantasy, an ultimate Thai cultural theme park.

Lastly, I hope this meeting is a great success and all delegates have a pleasant stay in Phuket. If there is anything that we could be of assistance with, you are welcome to contact our staff at the secretariat office. Thank you very much.

（文献来源：《粮农组织渔业和水产养殖业报告第950号：渔业委员会水产养殖分委员会第五届会议报告》，联合国粮食及农业组织，2010年，第38页。）

Reading Comprehension

Directions: In this part, you will have to go over the passage quickly and choose the best answer from the four choices marked A, B, C and D.

1. What does Somying Piumsombun on behalf of ?
   A. Minister of Agriculture and Cooperatives of Thailand
   B. the COFL Sub
   C. FAO
   D. the Department of Fisheries
2. Somying Piumsombunwish to extend her warm welcome to ________.
   A. FAO colleagues and all delegates from more than 50 countries for their participation in the Fifth Session of the COFI Sub
   B. Minister of Agriculture and Cooperatives of Thailand
   C. the COFL Sub
   D. the Department of Fisheries
3. Fisheries and aquaculture plays a vital role to ________.
   A. rural development
   B. the global and national economy in particular its contribution to food

security

C. not only to rural development but also to the global and national economy in particular its contribution to food security

D. the Department of Fisheries

4. As for aquaculture, Thailand has extensive experience in ________ which led to significant success during the past three decades.

A. marine shrimpculture

B. fish culture

C. cuttlefish culture

D. catfish culture

4.2 Opening Speech and Closing Speech

第二节　开幕词和闭幕词

Basic Knowledge

一、基础知识

Introduction

In some foreign affairs activities, leaders will announce the commencement of the activity by making a welcoming speech to the present people and introducing the activity, which is called the opening speech. When the affairs have nearly come to an end, the leaders will make a speech to evaluate and summarize the activity, which is called the closing speech.

（一）简介

开幕词是指在外交外事活动中，有关领导在活动开始时向参与人员宣布活动开始并发表的致词，多伴随着对参与人员的欢迎并简单介绍活动内容，同时表达期待。

闭幕词是指在外交外事活动即将结束时，有关领导人对该活动所做的带有评价性、总结性的讲话。它既是对活动基本内容的突出和强调，又是对该活动的总结。

Contents and Features

The Opening Speech usually includes the main gist of the activity that follows. Additionally, the relevant issues of the activity are mentioned to make it go well. Lastly, it expresses the warm welcome to those who are present. Generally speaking, the closing speech recalls the whole activity and gives an overall evaluation of it.

（二） 内容和特点

开幕词和闭幕词在内容与特点上既有相似之处，又有各自的差异。

开幕词的内容大致如下：首先，要求阐明活动主旨及其指导思想并说明活动基本程序；同时，提出活动注意事项；其次，以引导活动围绕既定主题和议程顺利进行；最后，简单表达对参与人员的欢迎以及对活动顺利进行的期待。

开幕词主要有如下特点：

1. 指导性。开幕词中通常阐述该外交外事活动召开的目的、意义、指导思想及中心任务。

2. 提示性。开幕词中一般都明确地宣布活动的主要议程，点明活动的主要精神，使参与人员心中有数，便于积极主动参与。

3. 鼓动性。在开幕词中，领导人以充满激情的语言调动参与人员的热情和积极性。

闭幕词主要对活动的基本情况进行回顾和总结，并对活动进行较为全面的评价，其特点主要有：

1. 总结性。闭幕词实际上是对活动的基本情况进行回顾和总结。

2. 评价性。闭幕词应对活动进行全面的评价，充分肯定活动所取得的成绩．正确评价活动的基本精神及由此产生的影响。

Writing Requirements

Both the opening and the closing speeches should stick to the point. The former should show warm welcome to create an atmosphere of friendliness and joyfulness. The latter should give a fair and overall evaluation of the activity. Both of them include such parts as title, signature, time, address, body and concluding remarks.

(三) 写作要求

开幕词既要有对会议或活动意义等方面的阐述，又要对与会者表示欢迎，所以感情要真挚，用语要礼貌。为了更好地达到效果，致词人要根据开幕式的场景和气氛起草与调整开幕词。其篇幅不宜过长，以免影响后面的议程。

开幕词的书写格式分为标题、署名和时间、称谓、正文、结语五部分。

1. 标题

(1) 由会议或者活动名称、文种组成，如“在×××会议上的开幕词”。

(2) 由致词人、会议或者活动名称、文种组成，如“×××在××××大会上的开幕词”。

2. 署名和时间

在标题下一行居中位置写上致词人的姓名，再下一行居中写致词时间。

3. 称谓

称谓是对与会者的统称，一般要写“同志们”“女士们”“先生们”。称谓后面加冒号。

4. 正文

正文主要是宣布会议或者活动开始，交代名称和内容，介绍出席的单位和领导人员。简要阐释组织者的初衷、会议或者活动的意义及其开展原则、影响。如果议程过多，可不在开幕词中一一列出。

5. 结语

开幕式的结语一般有两种，一种是直接宣布开幕，另一种是以祝颂语结束，如“预祝大会圆满成功”。

闭幕词具有总结性，所以起草闭幕词时语言要高度概括、简明精炼；对会议或者活动的总结、评价要合理，符合事实，不得任意拔高。其书写格式分为标题、署名和时间、称谓、正文、结语五部分。

1. 标题

会议或者活动名称＋文种，例如“在×××会议上的闭幕词”。

致词人＋会议或活动名称＋文种，例如“×××在×××大会上的闭幕词”。

2. 署名和时间

闭幕词在标题下一行居中位置写上致词人的姓名，再下一行居中写致词时间。

3. 称谓

称谓是对与会者的统称，一般是“同志们”“女士们”“先生们”等称呼。称谓后面加冒号。

4. 正文

正文中主要对会议或活动做出概括、总结，提出贯彻大会精神的要求和希望，可适当列举会议或者活动的成绩、成果等。

5. 结语

闭幕式的结语比较简单，通常直接宣布闭幕，如“现在，我宣布×××会议圆满闭幕!”。

（柏莹、王玥、王莫楠、芮念直、金晶，2011）

Case Studies

二、案例分析

案例一

IOC President's Speech at the Closing Ceremony of the Games of the XXIX Olympiad

24 August 2008

Dear Chinese Friends,

Tonight, we come to the end of 16 glorious days which we will cherish forever.

Thank you to the people of China, all the wonderful volunteers and BOCOG!

Through these Games, the world learned more about China, and China learned more about the world. Athletes from 204 National Olympic Committees came to these dazzling venues and awed us with their talent.

New stars were born. Stars from past Games amazed us again. We shared their joys and their tears, and we marveled at their ability. We will long remember the achievements we witnessed here.

As we celebrate the success of these Games, let us together wish the best for the talented athletes who will soon participate in the Paralympic Games. They also inspire us.

To the athletes tonight: You were true role models. You have shown us the unifying power of sport. The Olympic spirit lives in the warm embrace of competitive rivals from nations in conflict. Keep that spirit alive when you return home.

These were truly exceptional Games!

And now, in accordance with tradition, I declare the Games of the XXIX

Olympiad closed, and I call upon the youth of the world to assemble four years from now in London to celebrate the Games of the ××× Olympiad.

Thank you!

（文献来源：https: //www. olympic. org/news，检索日期：2015 年 3 月 15 日。）

Analysis

This is the closing speech for 2008 Beijing Olympic Games. It starts with thanks to China, followed by the retrospect of the past 16 days of games. Finally it announces that 2008 Beijing Olympic Games goes perfectly as expected and looks forward to London Olympic Games in 2012.

案例二

温家宝总理在第 110 届中国进出口商品交易会开幕式暨
中国加入世界贸易组织 10 周年论坛上的讲话
2011 年 10 月 14 日，广州

各位来宾，各位朋友，
女士们，先生们：

今天我们欢聚一堂，共同庆祝第 110 届中国进出口商品交易会（广交会）隆重开幕。我对各位嘉宾表示热烈欢迎，对长期以来为中国外贸事业发展做出贡献的各界人士表示崇高敬意！

广交会是中国政府在 1957 年创办的。50 多年来，广交会顺应时势变化，不断创新办展理念和办展方式，不断优化参展企业和参展商品，始终保持着旺盛的生命力和蓬勃的发展势头，成为中国历史最久、规模最大、声誉最佳的国际著名展会，成为中国对外贸易发展的缩影。一部广交会的历史，就是一部生动的中华人民共和国对外开放史。

展望未来，随着中国经济快速发展和改革开放不断推进，广交会面临更加广阔的发展前景。我们相信，广交会一定会办得更具特色、更上水平、更有成效，为促进我国对外贸易发展做出更大的贡献。

女士们，先生们：

再过两个月，我们就将迎来中国加入世贸组织10周年，这是中国对外开放进程中值得纪念的大事。如果说创办广交会是中国向世界打开了一扇窗，那么加入世贸组织就是中国向世界开启了一扇门；如果说创办广交会是中国向世界伸出一只手，那么加入世贸组织就是中国拥抱整个世界。

加入世贸组织10年来，中国的面貌发生了重大变化，中国对外经贸关系发生了重大变化，中国在世界大家庭中的地位和作用也发生了重大变化。回顾这10年历史，我们可以得出三个重要结论：

第一，中国是说话算数的国家，兑现了加入世界贸易组织时做出的郑重承诺。

10年来，我们全面履行诺言，逐步降低进口产品的关税税率，取消所有进口配额、许可证等非关税措施，全面放开对外贸易经营权，大幅降低外资准入门槛。中国关税总水平由15.3%降至9.8%，远远低于发展中国家的平均水平；中国服务贸易开放部门达到100个，接近发达国家的水平。

我们在扩大市场开放的同时，还致力于提高对外开放政策的稳定性、透明度和可预见性。10年来，中央政府共清理各种法律法规和部门规章2300多件，地方政府共清理地方性政策和法规19万多件，使国内涉外经济法律法规与我国加入世贸组织承诺相一致。

第二，中国是勇于担当的国家，积极承担着与自身发展水平相称的国际责任。

10年来，中国坚定支持世贸组织多哈回合谈判，积极参与国际宏观经济政策协调，参与20国集团等全球经济治理机制建设，推动国际金融体系改革，以实际行动反对贸易保护主义。在国际金融危机蔓延的时候，我国及时实施强有力的内需刺激政策，组织30多个大型采购团赴海外采购，我国进口和对外投资加快增长，为世界经济复苏做出了重要贡献。中国是最早制定并实施《应对气候变化国家方案》的发展中国家，也是近年来节能减排力度最大的国家之一。中国认真落实联合国千年发展目标，是全球唯一提前实现贫困人口减半的国家，并根据自身能力积极开展对外援助。近10年累计对外提供各类援款1700多亿元人民币，免除50个重债穷国近300亿元人民币到期债务，承诺对最不发达国家95%以上的输华产品实行零关税，为173个发展中国家和13个地区性国际组织培训各类人员6万多名，显著增强了受援国的自主发展能力。

第三，中国是致力于共同发展的国家，始终奉行平等互利、合作共赢的对外开放政策。

加入世贸组织对中国的积极影响是巨大而深远的。最显著的是，极大地促进了我国开放型经济发展，提升了我国经济的整体竞争力。10年来，中国货物贸易额由世界第六位上升到第二位，其中出口跃居第一位；累计吸收外商直接投资7595亿美元，居发展中国家首位；对外直接投资年均增长40%以上，2010年当年已达688亿美元，居世界第五位。各个产业在激烈的国际竞争中经受了考验。加入世贸组织给中国人民带来许多看得见、摸得着的好处，更重要的是开阔了人们的视野，改变了人们的思想观念，促进了中国体制改革和制度创新，大大增强了中国发展的内在动力。

中国加入世贸组织也为世界各国带来了实实在在的利益。这10年，中国每年平均进口7500亿美元的商品，相当于为贸易伙伴创造1400多万个就业岗位。在华外商投资企业累计汇出利润2617亿美元，年均增长30%。中国对外投资企业聘用当地员工接近80万人，每年在当地纳税超过100亿美元。中国物美价廉的商品为国外消费者带来了巨大实惠，由于进口中国商品，美国消费者过去10年共节省开支6000多亿美元，欧盟每个家庭每年可以节省开支300欧元。

实践证明，中国扩大对外开放，惠及13亿中国人民，也惠及世界各国人民。中国的发展，是和平的发展、开放的发展、合作的发展、共赢的发展。中国加入世贸组织大家庭，是中国的成功，也是世界的成功！

女士们，先生们：

中国对外开放30多年来的实践告诉我们：只有开放兼容，国家才能富强，人民才能过上幸福美好的生活。我们要倍加珍惜和维护对外开放的成果，将对外开放贯穿于我国现代化建设全过程，奋力把对外开放的伟大事业推向前进，为建设一个富强民主文明和谐的国家、为世界的繁荣发展和文明进步不懈努力！

谢谢大家！

（文献来源：中国商务部网站，http: //www. mofcom. gov. cn，检索日期：2015 年 1 月 20 日。）

分析概要

本文是国务院前总理温家宝在第 110 届中国出口商品交易会开幕式上的讲话，从其结构上看，分为称谓、正文、结语等部分。正文先对各位嘉宾表示热烈欢迎，后简单介绍会议内容并给予期待。本次讲话同时也是一个关于中国加入世界贸易组织 10 周年的讲话，并阐述了未来的挑战和机遇。

Supplementary Readings
三、拓展阅读

请分别阅读以下闭幕词和开幕词，回答问题。

在香港特别行政区筹委会预委会第二次全会上的闭幕词
（一九九三年十二月十一日）
钱其琛

在预委会本次全体会议召开之前，内地有一件大事，那就是《邓小平文选》第三卷的发表。在预委会第一次全体会议上，我曾宣读了邓小平在一九八二年九月二十四日同撒切尔夫人的谈话，这篇谈话已经编入了《邓小平文选》第三卷，题为《我们对香港的基本立场》。与这篇谈话同时编进《邓小平文选》发表的邓小平关于香港问题的谈话还有另外八篇。这些谈话是有关中国政府对香港问题的基本立场和方针、政策的经典性论述。有些谈话是对英国人说的，有些谈话是对香港同胞，包括基本法起草委员会说的。完整、准确地理解邓小平代表中国政府所阐明的对香港问题的立场和方针政策，对于了解中英之间就香港问题进行谈判的情况，对于预委会完成全国人大赋予的使命，做好对香港恢复行使主权的准备工作，都是十分重要的。

香港问题是个历史遗留问题。通过三个不平等条约，英国占领这块本属中国的领土已达一百多年。考虑香港的前途问题，必须从这个基本事实出发，前提是中国必须对香港恢复行使主权。对这个毋庸置疑的问题，英方却在香港前途问题谈判一开始就做文章，先是提出“三个条约有效论”，继而又提出以主权换治权的主张，实际上“三个条约有效论”是为主权换治权铺路的。邓小平对撒切尔夫人的谈话就是针对这个问题而来的。他明确地告诉撒切尔夫人，我们要解决的是三个问题：一是就中国对香港恢复行使主权达成协议；二是中国在恢复行使主权后对香港采取的政策，也就是怎样管理香港；三是过渡时期的安排，也就是为我们对香港恢复行使主权创造条件。这三个方面构成香港主权回归的完整意义。然而直至一九八三年的第四轮会谈，英方仍然坚持要在一九九七年后继续管治香港，致使谈判毫无进展。

针对这一情况，一九八三年九月邓小平在会见英国前首相希思时明确指出，英国想用主权来换治权是行不通的。他正告英方改变态度，以免到一九八四年九月中国不得不单方面宣布解决香港问题的方针政策。这样英方才在第五、第六轮谈判中确认不再坚持英国管治，也不谋求任何形式的共管，并表示理解中国的计划是建立在一九九七年后整个香港的主权和管治权应该归还中国这一前提的基础上。中英谈判的主要障碍自此开始排除。

后来邓小平在谈到这段历史时说，“她（撒切尔夫人）坚持历史上的条约按国际法仍然有效，一九九七年后英国要继续管理香港。我跟她说，主权问题是不能谈判的，中国一九九七年要收回整个香港。”邓小平所说的“整个香港”绝不仅仅是个地理概念，而是一个主权概念，就是说，三分之一或二分之一的主权不行，必须是完整的主权。进入过渡时期后半段以来，特别是近年来在香港发生的风波曲折足以说明，英国谋求一九九七年后对香港的“治权”的企图实际上仍然存在。从“两局共识”到“居英权计划”，直至那个“三违反”的“政改方案”，诸如此类，有哪一个不是企图把英国的影响长久地保持下去？作为预委会委员，我们对此应有清醒的认识和足够的思想准备。

我们对香港的政策是以“一国两制”为基础，它主要包括以下四个方面：一是中国对香港恢复行使主权并同时设立特别行政区，直辖于中央人民政府，这是解决香港的法律地位问题；二是中央授权香港特别行政区实行高度自治，由香港当地人自己管理，这是解决管理权和由谁来掌权的问题；三是香港的原有社会、经济制度不变，生活方式不变，法律基本不变，这是解决香港的基本制度和政策问题；四是保持香港国际金融中心、自由港的地位，这也是从香港的实际需要出发，为保持香港的稳定繁荣所必需的。我们之所以要对香港实行一系列特殊政策，就是为了实现既要对香港恢复行使主权，又要保持香港繁荣稳定这一总体目标。正如邓小平所说，“保持香港的繁荣，我们希望取得英国的合作。但这不是说，香港继续保持繁荣必须在英国的管辖之下才能实现。香港继续保持繁荣，根本上取决于中国收回主权后，在中国的管辖之下实行适合于香港的制度”。我们的政策通过联合声明和基本法，不仅为香港同胞所接受，而且受到国际社会的赞赏。

基本法颁布后，英国政府曾公开表示，这是一部值得推荐的法律。这些说明，我们对香港的政策为中英在香港问题上长期合作提供了基础。然而，合作的基础有了，是不是合作的问题统统解决了呢？并没有。因为总有人不甘心退出历史舞台，总想制造一些混乱。在这里我只举一个例子。一九八四年七月三十一日邓小平曾当面对英国的外交大臣指出了我们不希望在过渡时期出现的五种具体情况，其中他谈到，希望港英政府不要在过渡时期自搞一套班子，将来强加于香港特别行政区政府。事实让邓小平不幸言中：在联合声明明确规定在过渡时期的后半段，中英双方“有必要进行更密切的合作”，“审议为一九九七年顺利过渡所要采取的措施”之后，在基本法和全国人大的有关决定对香港的政治体制和民主发展做出了明确规定之后，在中英两国外长就有关的政制安排达成谅解和协议之后，还是有人提出“三违反”的“政改方案”，这不就是“人为制造的混乱”吗？所以，邓小平又讲，“我担心的是今后十五年过渡时期如何过渡好，担心在这个时期会出现很大的混乱，而且这些混乱是人为的。这当中不光有外国人，也有中国人，而主要的是英国人。”这确实是我们需要高度警惕的。当然，我们还是希望通过合作来制止混乱，把可能发生的波动减少到最小的程度。但是如果合作不下去，我们也不会坐视香港发生混乱。我们要按照基本法的规定，做好各项必要的准备工作，坚持“一国两制”的方针，不折不扣地贯彻基本法。这就是我们预委会要负起的责任。

我们肩负的责任重大，尤其是香港同胞更是责无旁贷。再有三年多一点的时间，我们便要把香港接过来，交给香港人自己去管理，而且还要让它继续繁荣发展下去。邓小平早在一九八四年就讲过，“要相信香港的中国人能治理好香港。不相信中国人有能力管好香港，这是老殖民主义遗留下来的思想状态”。邓小平又说，“香港过去的繁荣，主要是以中国人为主体的香港人干出来的”，“香港人是能治理好香港的，要有这个自信心”。我们今天所从事的事业，是一项可告慰先人、可造福子孙的事业。正在振兴的中华民族，日益兴旺发达的中华人民共和国，给了我们义无反顾地去进行这项事业的力量和勇气。此志不可攀，其势不可挡。我们坚信，“一国两制”的政策一定能在香港开花结果；基本法规定的各项方针政策必将得到贯彻，基本法所规定的各项目标必将实现；我们的神圣使命将得到一切爱好和平与进步事业的国家和人民的支持；一九九七年后的香港一定更加繁荣发达！

我深信通过我们的工作，并随着九七年的临近，将有越来越多的人自觉地站在维护香港的繁荣稳定和平稳过渡一边，或直接或间接地参与到筹备成立香港特别行政区的各项准备工作中来。有了这些有利的条件，我们就能够扎实、紧凑、有效地完成各项准备工作。

（文献来源：戴舟：《邓小平理论与当代中国》（第四卷），红旗出版社 1998 年版，第 3624 - 3626 页。）

Reading Comprehension

Directions: Please give brief answers to the following questions.

1. 请简述该闭幕词的主要内容。
2. 从格式上看，该闭幕词是否符合要求？有无需要补充的地方？
3. 从内容上看，该闭幕词是否完整？
4. 分析该闭幕词对于当时解决“香港问题”的意义。

粮农组织渔业和水产养殖部助理总干事的
代表 Kevern Cochrane 先生的开幕词

Your Excellency Mr Theera Wongsamut, Minister of Agriculture and Cooperatives, Distinguished Ms. Somying Piumsombun, Director-General of the Department of Fisheries Kingdom of Thailand, Distinguished Delegates, Colleagues, Ladies and Gentlemen,

It gives me much pleasure and is an honour to be with you today on this auspicious occasion of the fifth Session of the FAO COFI Sub-Committee on Aquaculture. As you may know, Mr. Ichiro Nomura, our previous Assistant Director-General, retired at the end of July and his successor has not yet been appointed. In the interim, I am pleased to be able to say a few words on behalf of the Fisheries and Aquaculture Department and of the Director-General, Mr. Jacques Diouf allow me first, to convey to you his warm greetings and best wishes for a constructive and fruitful meeting. At this juncture, I would like to pay a special tribute to the Government of the Kingdom of Thailand for hosting this important meeting in this charming city of Phuket. It is a clear indication that the Government of Thailand places great importance on the development of aquaculture, not only in your own country, Thailand, but also to the sector's sustainable development throughout the world. I should also like to convey a warm welcome to all Delegates representing FAO member countries and represe-ntatives of various Inter-Governmental Organizations and interna-tional non-governmental organizations. We see in your active and continued participation in this and other sessions of the Sub-Committee, a clear expression of commitment to ensuring the achievement of the shared and agreed objectives, not only of combating hunger and poverty, but also of enhancing economic and social conditions through responsible aquaculture development worldwide. A commitment of this nature is of utmost impor- tance if the world is to feed its ever growing population and improve the livelihoods of communities and aquaculture is to play its full role in achieving this. When we consider that the human population of the world is projected to grow from just under 7 billion today to over 9 billion in 2050, the essential role of aquaculture in ensuring food security now and in the future becomes even clearer.

Information at our disposal reveals that in 2008. the sector produced 52. 5 million tonnes of fishery products, which represented about 37 percent of the fishery products produced worldwide and contributed nearly 46 percent of the world's fish production for human consumption. The total value was more than 98 billion US dollars. In addition, close to 16 million tonnes of algae were produced by this sector, value at more than 7 billion US dollars.

Though the information on trade of aquaculture products is often weak, there are credible indications that important quantities of fish from farms move into global trade, bringing significant amounts of money into national economies.

Further, a recent FAO estimate of employment in aquaculture indicates that, in 2008, the sector provided over 30 million full-time-equivalent jobs, including about 21 million on-farm and 9 million off-farm positions.

Distinguished Delegates, Ladies and Gentlemen, I do not wish to anticipate the Agenda of the meeting, but I should like to call your attention to the fundamental problem we face today: aquaculture has made laudable efforts to meet the growing demand for fish and seafood products in a sustainable way, but there are substantial challenges ahead of us. Many of these are due to be discussed over the next five days.

The current levels of exploitation of wild fish resources are at their maximum and in some cases above it. There is therefore no scope for an increase in capture fishery production to respond to the increasing demands and needs for fish for the ever-growing world population. Aquaculture will have to fill this void.

To do so, because of the scarcity of inland environmental capacity for aquaculture development including the availability of land and water, more and more sea and ocean resources will have to be utilized for aquaculture purposes. Coastal areas suitable and available for aquaculture development are also limited and the expansion of aquaculture operations into the sea might require adjustments in the way the sector is governed.

Other serious obstacles to aquaculture expansion are likely to come from climate change and climatic uncertainty. Both will need adaptation and mitigation strategies, which should include collection, dissemination and exchange of information.

Through its globalized hygiene and traceability requirements, domestic and international trade could also influence the pace at which the sector develops, and also how it develops. This implies that the issue of certification of aquaculture products is and will remain important in the years ahead; it needs to be addressed, and this Sub-Committee is making a valuable contribution in this regard.

（文献来源：《粮农组织渔业和水产养殖业报告第950号：渔业委员会水产养殖分委员会第五届会议报告》，联合国粮食及农业组织，2010年，第36－37页。）

Reading Comprehension

Directions: In this part, you will have to go over the passage quickly and choose the best answer from the four choices marked A, B, C and D.

1. What does this opening speech mainly about?
   A. marine shrimp culture
   B. on this auspicious occasion of the fifth Session of the FAO COFI Sub-Committee on Aquaculture
   C. the global and national economy in particular its contribution to food security
   D. the reform of the Department of Fisheries
2. What is this speaker on behalf of?
   A. the Fisheries and Aquaculture Department and of the Director
   B. Minister of Agriculture and Cooperatives of Thailand
   C. the Department of Fisheries
   D. the COFL Sub
3. The speaker conveys a warm welcome to ________ .
   A. all Delegates representing FAO member countries
   B. representatives of various Inter-Governmental Organizations
   C. International Governmental Organizations and non-governmental organizations
   D. all of the A, B and C
4. What leads to more and more sea and ocean resources utilized for aquaculture purposes in the future?
   A. The lack of protection of sea environment
   B. the pollution of the sea
   C. The scarcity of inland environmental capacity for aquaculture development including the availability of land and water
   D. all of the A, B, and C

4.3 Toasts

第三节 祝酒词

Basic Knowledge

一、基础知识

Introduction

Toasts are oral statements made by state leaders or diplomats of higher rank on official or social occasions, but they are still one type of significant documents in diplomacy. Most of the toasts were actually well-prepared before the statements. Even though some of them are improvised, they would be recorded later to be reserved.

（一）简介

祝酒词是国家领导人或高级外交官在官方或社交活动中所做的口头讲话。它们虽是口头讲话，但也是一种重要的外交文件。因为事实上，大部分祝酒词是由讲话人在讲话场合宣读的事先准备好的书面文件。即使是即席的讲话，如果需要，它们也将被记录下来，因而也成为文件。

除纯属礼节性的目的以外，外交讲演和祝酒词也是政治家或外交家阐述他的国家关于各种涉及双边或国际关系问题的观点、立场和政策的重要手段。讲演比祝酒词一般说来要更正式些和更有实质内容（祝酒词只用于宴会或招待会）。但祝酒词的重要性主要决定于它们的实质内容、场合和讲话人。

祝酒词没有严格的格式，但在起草时仍有一般规则可循。此外，像外交本身一样，起草祝酒词也是一种技巧和艺术。

（黄金祺，2004）

Contents and Features

The toast is one of the important ways to receive distinguished guests on the banquet. Generally, both the host and the guest should give toasts. The former focuses more on welcoming the guests and the latter should express their heartfelt thanks and best wishes.

（二）内容和特点

宴会上祝酒，是招待宾客的重要礼仪之一。一般来说，主宾均要致祝酒词。祝酒词以酒为媒介，加之以热烈、真诚的语言，会为宴请平添许多友好的气氛。一般来说，主方的祝酒词侧重于向来宾表示欢迎；客方的祝酒词主要是表示对主方的谢忱、祝福、庆贺等。有时出于某种礼仪需要，也可在祝酒词中做出符合宴会氛围的深沉、委婉或幽默的表达。

（肖莉，2007）

其特点主要有：

1. 感情真挚、坦诚而热烈

“祝贺”是一种“言情”方式，既然要“言情”，就应该热烈奔放、热情洋溢，给人以如沐春风的温煦感；否则，那种冷冰冰、干巴巴、走过场式的致词是很难获得对方认可的。

2. 评价适度，恰如其分

一般说来，对对方做出的评价，要适度，要恰如其分，不可故意拔高、无限升华，以免造成“虚情假意”之嫌。

3. 篇幅简短，语言精练

礼仪“仪式”毕竟不是开大会，致词一般比较简短，应语言精练，“文约旨丰”，言简意赅。

（戴盛才，2011）

Writing Requirements

Toast, generally, includes such parts as title, address, body and concluding remarks.

Consider the following suggestions:

1. Keep the toast short. If the dinner is awaiting people on plates in front of them, show mercy and speak briefly.
2. Use a phrase that brings people into the toast, something like "This is the moment when we honor the team's successes in 2010…" or "Please join me in raising your glass in celebration of our…"
3. Use humor if you can, but avoid sarcasm. A toast is a feel-good message. It should not bite anyone.
4. Avoid references to people and events that some guests, such as spouses, will not be recognize. Identify people with phrases such as "our chairman, David Blake" and "our biggest client, ××× Company".
5. Feel free to use or build on other toasts or famous quotations, like this: "Henry David Thoreau said that it is a characteristic of wisdom not to do desperate things. I am proud to acknowledge that we acted wisely this year, even in the face of tremendous challenges."

（三）写作要求

祝酒词由标题、称谓、正文、主体、结语五部分构成。

1. 标题

书面型标题可以直接写为《祝词》《祝酒词》等，也可以由致词人姓名、酒宴名称和文种构成，如《×××在××上的祝酒词》《×××在××宴会上的祝词》等。

2. 称谓

称谓根据赴宴者的身份来定，为了表示热情和亲切、友好之意，名前面可以加修饰语“亲爱的”“尊敬的”“尊贵的”等。

3. 正文

正文的开头部分用来表达欢迎、问候或感谢之情。书写时，应注明致词人（或代表谁）是在什么情况下，向出席者祝酒。

4. 主体

主体部分根据宴请的对象、宴会的性质，简略地表述主人必要的想法、观点、立场和意见，既可以追述已经获得的成绩，也可以畅叙友情发展的历史，还可以展望未来。

5. 结语

结语又称为祝福语、祝愿语、祝酒语，可用“让我们为……干杯”或以“为了……让我们干杯”表达礼节性的祝愿。

（肖莉，2007）

Case Studies
二、案例分析

案例一

Toast Speech by Richard Nixon

（A toast given by president Nixon on his first visit to China in 1972）

Mr. Prime Minister and all of your distinguished guests this evening:

On behalf of all of your American guests, I wish to thank you for the incomparably hospitality for which the Chinese people are justly famous throughout the world. I particularly want to pay tribute, not only to those who prepared the magnificent dinner, but also to those who have provided the splendid music. Never have I heard American music played better in a foreign land.

Mr. Prime Minister, I wish to thank you for your very gracious and eloquent remarks. At this very moment, through the wonder of telecommunications, more people are seeing and hearing what we say than on any other such occasion in the whole history of the world. Yet, what we say here will not be long remembered. What we do here can change the world.

As you said in your toast, the Chinese people are a great people, the American people are a great people. If our two peoples are enemies, the future of this world we share together is dark indeed. But if we can find common ground to work together, the chance for world peace is immeasurably increased.

In the spirit of frankness which I hope will characterize our talks this week, let us recognize at the outset these points: We have at times in the past been enemies. We have great differences today. What brings us together is that we have common interests which transcend those differences. As we discuss our differences, neither of us will compromise our principles. But while we cannot close the gulf between us, we can try to bridge it so that we may be able to talk across it.

So, let us, in these next five days, start a long march together, not in lockstep, but on different roads leading to the same goal, the goal of building a world structure of peace and justice in which all may stand together with equal dignity and in which each nation, large or small, has a right to determine its own form of government, free of outside interference or domination. The world watches. The world listens. The world waits to see what we will do. What is the world? In a personal sense, I think of my eldest daughter whose birthday is today. As I think of her, I think of all the children in the world, in Asia, in Africa, in Europe, in the Americas, most of whom were born since the date of the foundation of the People's Republic of China.

What legacy shall we leave our children? Are they destined to die for the hatreds which have plagued the old world, or are they destined to live because we had the vision to build a new world?

There is no reason for us to be enemies. Neither of us seeks the territory of the other; neither of us seeks domination over the other; neither of us seeks to stretch out our hands and rule the world.

Chairman Mao has written, "So many deeds cry out to be done, and always urgently; the world rolls on, Time presses. Ten thousand years are too long, seize the day, seize the hour!"

This is the hour. This is the day for our two peoples to rise to the heights of greatness which can build a better world.

In that spirit, I ask all of you present to join me in raising your glasses to Chairman Mao, to Prime Minister Chou, and to the friendship of the Chinese and American people which can lead to friendship and peace for all people in the world.

(文献来源：方舒："尼克松的祝酒词"，《领导文萃》1996 年第 1 期，第 52 - 53 页。)

Analysis

The toast was addressed when Richard Nixon visited China in 1972. In terms of structure, the toast is just like others, which was addressed by ex-president of United States to Chinese leaders. It expressed the good will for the future of Sino-US relationship and the world peace and prosperity. Meanwhile, when we read between lines, it shows that it is a response to another toast.

案例二

周总理在欢迎尼克松总统的宴会上的祝酒词
(一九七二年二月二十一日)

总统先生，尼克松夫人，
女士们，先生们，
同志们，朋友们：

首先，我高兴地代表毛泽东主席和中国政府向尼克松总统和夫人，以及其他的美国客人们，表示欢迎。同时，我也想利用这个机会代表中国人民向远在大洋彼岸的美国人民致以亲切的问候。

尼克松总统应中国政府的邀请，前来我国访问，使两国领导人有机会直接会晤，谋求两国关系正常化，并就共同关心的问题交换意见，这是符合中美两国人民愿望的积极行动，这在中美两国关系史上是一个创举。

美国人民是伟大的人民。中国人民是伟大的人民。我们两国人民一向是友好的。由于大家都知道的原因，两国人民之间的来往中断了二十多年。现在，经过中美双方的共同努力，友好来往的大门终于打开了。目前，促使两国关系正常化，争取和缓紧张局势，已成为中美两国人民强烈的愿望。人民，只有人民，才是创造世界历史的动力。我们相信，我们两国人民这种共同愿望，总有一天是要实现的。

中美两国的社会制度根本不同，在中美两国政府之间存在着巨大的分歧。但是，这种分歧不应当妨碍中美两国在互相尊重主权和领土完整、互不侵犯、互不干涉内政、平等互利和和平共处五项原则的基础上建立正常的国家关系，更不应该导致战争。中国政府早在一九五五年就公开声明，中国人民不要同美国打仗，中国政府愿意坐下来同美国政府谈判，这是我们一贯奉行的方针。我们注意到尼克松总统在来华前的讲话中也谈到，“我们必须做的事情是寻找某种办法使我们可以有分歧而又不成为战争中的敌人”。我们希望，通过双方坦率地交换意见，弄清楚彼此之间的分歧，努力寻找共同点，我们两国的关系能够有一个新的开始。

最后，我建议：

为尼克松总统和夫人的健康，

为其他美国客人们的健康，

为在座的所有朋友们和同志们的健康，

为中美两国人民之间的友谊，

干杯！

（文献来源：冬梅：《中美关系资料选编（1971.7－1981.7）》，时事出版社1982年版，第20－21页。）

分析概要

这篇祝酒词恰恰是上一篇祝酒词所回复的致词。和英文祝酒词一样，中文祝酒词也分为标题、称谓、正文、结语等部分。学习时应注意比较中英文祝酒词之间的异同。

Supplementary Readings
三、拓展阅读

请仔细阅读以下两则祝酒词，回答问题。

为日中友好迈出新的一步
——在周恩来总理欢迎宴会上的祝酒词
（1972 年 9 月 25 日）
田中角荣

尊敬的周恩来总理阁下以及在座的各位先生：

这次，我能够应周恩来总理阁下的邀请，以日本国总理大臣的身份，踏上我国邻邦中国的国土，感到非常高兴。今天又举行如此盛大的晚宴欢迎我们，我心中感到非常温暖，对于有关方面各位先生的关照，谨表示深切的谢意。

这次访问，我是由东京直飞北京的，我再一次深深地感到日中两国是一衣带水的近邻。两国不仅在地理上如此相近，而且有着长达两千年丰富多彩的交往的历史。

然而，遗憾的是过去几十年之间，日中关系经历了不幸的过程。其间，我国给中国国民添了很大的麻烦，我对此再次表示深切的反省之意。第二次世界大战后，日中关系仍继续处于不正常、不自然的状态，我们不得不坦率地承认这个历史事实。但是，我们不能永远沉沦在过去的暗淡的死胡同里。我认为，现在日中两国的领导人为了明天进行会谈是重要的。为了明天进行会谈，也就是为了亚洲乃至世界和平和繁荣这一共同的目标，进行坦率而有诚意的会谈。我这次前来此地，正是为了这一目的。我们愿望，同伟大的中国及其国民之间能够建立起睦邻友好关系，两国能够一面互相尊重对方同其友好国家的关系，一面为亚洲乃至世界和平和繁荣做出贡献。

不言而喻，日中之间政治信仰和社会制度是不同的。但是，我认为，尽管如此，日中双方建立睦邻友好关系并在平等互利的基础上，加强交流，尊重相互的立场，进行合作，是可能的。

为要把日中之间的睦邻友好关系建立在坚固的基础上，实现邦交正常化是绝对必要的。当然，双方有各自的基本立场和特殊情况。但是我相信，哪怕双方的立场和意见存在着一些小异，日中双方根据求大同和互谅互让的精神，克服意见分歧，达成协议是可能的。我愿意完成这一重任，在悠久的日中友好的道路上迈出新的一步。

最后，我借主人的酒提议：同周恩来总理阁下以及各位先生一起举杯，为毛泽东主席阁下的幸福健康，为周恩来总理阁下的身体健康和工作顺利，为日中两国国民的永久的友好和亚洲的和平、繁荣，干杯！

（文献来源：岳海翔、李树春著：《影响世界历史的经典演讲词赏析》，中共中央党校出版社 2013 年版，第 364－365 页。）

Reading Comprehension

Directions: Please give brief answers to the following questions.

1. 请简述该祝酒词的主要内容。
2. 从格式上看，该祝酒词是否符合要求？
3. 从内容上看，该祝酒词是否完整？
4. 分析该祝酒词对于当时中日关系的意义。

Toast Remarks at the State Banquet in Honour of President Sellapan Ramanathan of the Republic of Singapore

Presidential Guest House, Tshwane, 19 April 2007

Your Excellency, President S. R. Nathan and Mrs Urmila Nathan,
Your Excellency, Deputy President Phumzile Mlambo-Ngcuka,
Your Excellencies, Ministers and Deputy Ministers,
Your Excellencies, Ambassadors and High Commissioners,
Distinguished Guests,
Ladies and Gentlemen:

On behalf of the government and people of South Africa and on my own behalf, I wish to extend a warm welcome to you, Your Excellency, your wife and the entire delegation from the Republic of Singapore.

We are indeed highly honoured that Your Excellency has paid us a State Visit, further to strengthen the economic, political and cultural ties between our two peoples.

Despite the early onset of the winter season I am confident that Your Excellency and his delegation will find our people warm and most friendly and welcoming.

Your Excellency, when we asked you, in April 2005 during our State Visit to your beautiful country, to visit South Africa, we knew that you would not hesitate to reciprocate because the close relations between our two countries, our common commitment to the development of the countries of the South, to democracy and human rights, to peace and security in the world, defy the long distance and the turbulent seas that separate our countries.

We are indeed happy that you came to South Africa, because among other things, this has given us the opportunity further to strengthen our bilateral relations, especially to give better effect to the Memorandum of Understanding concerning

Bilateral Cooperation in areas such as Trade and Investment, Transport, Housing, Tourism, Maritime matters, Aviation, Academic Cooperation, Human Resource Development and Crime and Terrorism.

Your Excellency, our close economic relations are reflected by our trade figures which indicate that South Africa and Singapore's total trade rose by 50 percent with a value of R11, 3 billion during 2006 compared to 2005.

Further, we are confident that we will continue to pursue the objective of a Free Trade Agreement, working together with our Southern African Customs Union fellow-members. We will also work to finalise the Open Skies Agreement, the better to cement our already improving economic relations.

You will be proud, Your Excellency, that our relationship is both practical and mutually beneficial, as demonstrated, among others, by the fact that Straits Chemicals of Singapore has committed an estimated US $5 billion for investment at Coega, one of our Industrial Development Zone. Any outstanding matters in this regard will soon be addressed so as to finalise this project.

Your Excellency, I would like to thank you personally, as well as the government and people of Singapore for helping us to respond to one of the biggest challenges facing us, which is skills development. South Africa has benefited from the Singapore Cooperation Programme hosted by your Ministry of Foreign Affairs, which has trained almost 700 officials and other representatives from South Africa in a wide range of fields and interests.

……

Once again, I am very delighted that you, Your Excellency, your wife and your delegation have come to South Africa.

Ladies and Gentlemen: Please join me in a toast to the good health and prosperity of their Excellencies, President Sellapan Ramanathan and Mrs Urmila Ramanathan and to the ever-lasting friendship and cooperation between the wonderful peoples of Singapore and South Africa. To good health and happiness!

Thank you.

（文献来源：http: //www. unisa. ac. za/contents/colleges/docs/tm2007/tm0419. pdf, 检索日期：2016 年 4 月 12 日。）

Reading Comprehension

Directions: Please give brief answers to the following questions.

1. What is the main idea of this toast?
2. Can you generalize some basic features of the above toast?
3. How do you respond to this toast in written way?

4. 4 Exercises
课后练习

- **True or False**

Directions: Read the following sentences and decide whether they are true or false.

1. Speech documents are oral statements made by state leaders or diplomats of higher rank on official or social occasions.
2. A diplomatic speech has rigid forms.
3. Seeing-off speech will not be recorded.
4. In some foreign affairs activities, some leaders will announce the beginning of the activity by making a welcoming speech to the present people and introducing the activity, which is called the opening speech.
5. Toasts are oral statements made by state leaders or diplomats of higher rank on official or social occasions, but they are still the significant documents in diplomacy.
6. Toasts could be used on any occasions as long as concerned with the foreign affairs.

• Gap-filling

Directions: Complete each sentence with appropriate words.

1. (Speech Documents) their significance depends mainly on the importance of their ________, the ________ and the ________. Many speeches have become historic international documents.
2. In some foreign affairs activities, the leaders will announce the ________ of the activity by making a welcoming speech to the present people and in troducing the activity, which is called ________.
3. Toasts are ________ statements made by ________ or diplomats of ________ on official or social occasions.

• Multiple Choices

Directions: In this part there are 5 incomplete sentences. For each sentence there are four choices marked A, B, C and D. Choose the ONE answer that best completes the sentence.

1. In the formal occasion of the foreign affairs, ________ should play host to the foreign guest to make him feel at home, and the welcoming speech the host made is called welcoming speech.

   A. the host country　　B. the guest

   C. both the host and the guest　　D. neither the host or the guest
2. A diplomatic speech has no ________ forms.

   A. simple　　B. rigid

   C. official　　D. right
3. (The host and the guest) they both attend a farewell banquet. On this occasion, the host will address himself a seeing-off speech to show the clinging feeling and strengthen their friendship, which is called ________.

   A. seeing-off speech　　B. farewell speech

   C. goodbye speech　　D. either is OK
4. When the foreign affairs have nearly ________, the leaders will make a

speech to evaluate and summarize the activity; that is called the closing speech.

A. begun B. come to a key period

C. come to an end D. come to the middle

5. Speech documents are oral statements made by ________.

A. state leaders

B. state leaders or diplomats of higher rank on official or social occasions

C. the elected secretary

D. the spokesman of the foreign ministry

• Translation

Directions: translate the following sentences into the target language.

English-Chinese translation

1. And thank you for joining us as we host President Hu and the Chinese delegation, and as we pay tribute to the bonds between two great nations and two proud peoples.
2. President Hu, we have met today in a spirit of mutual respect: the United States--the oldest democracy in the world, and China—one of the oldest civilizations in the world.
3. Our 21 economies—our nearly 3 billion citizens—are looking to us to bring our economies closer, to increase exports, to expand trade and opportunity that creates jobs and economic growth.
4. And as a consequence, the Asia Pacific region is key to achieving my goal of doubling U. S. exports and creating new jobs.
5. What legacy shall we leave our children? Are they destined to die for the hatreds which have plagued the old world, or are they destined to live because we had the vision to build a new world?
6. Chairman Mao has written, "So many deeds cry out to be done, and always urgently; the world rolls on, Time presses. Ten thousand years

are too long, seize the day, seize the hour!"

7. On behalf of all of your American guests, I wish to thank you for the incomparably hospitality for which the Chinese people are justly famous throughout the world.

Chinese-English translation

1. 对于我们来说，刘少奇主席阁下的初次访问柬埔寨，是我们国家历史上的一件大事，全体高棉人民今天热情洋溢地加以庆祝，以为这是永远把我们两国连结在一起的亲如兄弟的友谊的新的光辉例证。

2. 我特别感到高兴的是，刘少奇主席阁下以及陪同他的高级人士的这次访问提供了新的机会，使我们能在作为我们之间的关系的特征的不寻常的坦率和友好气氛中，就我们两国共同关心的问题交换意见。

3. 展望未来，随着中国经济快速发展和改革开放不断推进，广交会面临更加广阔的发展前景。

4. 如果说创办广交会是中国向世界打开了一扇窗，那么加入世贸组织就是中国向世界开启了一扇门；如果说创办广交会是中国向世界伸出一只手，那么加入世贸组织就是中国拥抱整个世界。

5. 这种分歧不应当妨碍中美两国在互相尊重主权和领土完整、互不侵犯、互不干涉内政、平等互利和和平共处五项原则的基础上建立正常的国家关系。

6. 我们希望，通过双方坦率地交换意见，弄清楚彼此之间的分歧，努力寻找共同点，我们两国的关系能够有一个新的开始。

• Simulative Exercise

Suppose China is going to serve a state banquet for the country who intends to pay a state visit. Yet the two countries haven't established diplomatic relations. This visit is actually concerned with the establishment of the diplomatic relations. Please write a toast for that banquet.

5 Documents of Declaration
第五章 告启文书

Abstract

With the development of international relations, the meetings of state leaders become more and more frequent. After the conference, they often issue documents of declaration.

Declaration refers to the statement and announcement, which aims to inform public or explain related affairs. There are mainly two types of documents of declaration. One is statement, which is used to show position or attitude to certain matters or issues to society. The other is communiqué, a reported official document issued by party, government or public organizations to release public events or important decisions. It is one of the important practical documents frequently used by our party or country. Both statement and communiqué are classified as practical writing in foreign documents.

This chapter will introduce the definition, features, writing requirements and selected cases of diplomatic statement and communiqué. The purpose of this chapter is to facilitate the understanding of the two documents and improve the writing skills.

内容概览

随着国家关系的不断发展，国家领导人之间的会晤越来越频繁。一般在会晤之后，它们会发表一些告启类的文书。

告启是指陈述、告知的意思。告启文书指向公众宣布，说明事物的问题。在外交外事文书领域，告启文书有两种类型：一种是声明，声明是就有关事项或问题向社会表明自己立场、态度的应用文体；另一种是公报，公报是党政机关和人民团体公开发布重大事件或重要决定事项的报道性公文，是党和国家经常使用的重要文种。

本章将详细介绍外交声明和外交公报的定义、特点、写作要求，同时精选案例作为示范，旨在加强读者对这两种文书的了解，提高相关人员关于这两种文书的写作水平。

5.1 Statement
第一节 声明

Basic Knowledge
一、基础知识

Introduction

Statement is one kind of documents of declaration. It is a formal document issued by government, party, groups, foreign institutions, media or their president and representatives for an international issue or event. The purpose of it is to express their standpoint, view or advice, showing their reflection, motion or policy to related questions or events.

In diplomatic practice, a statement is generally issued by a government. Sometimes, it can also be issued personally by an influential leader (Stalin and Mao Zedong, for instance, used to issue personal statements; the Presidents and Secretaries of the United States have acted likewise.)

（一）简介

外交声明通常是由国家、政府、政党、团体、外交机构、新闻单位等或其领导人、代表就某一国际问题或事件发表自己的立场、观点、态度和主张，表明其对相关问题或事件的反应、情绪、政策等的正式外交文件。

（范浩鸣、阳晴、黄宏丰、韦韩克等，2008）

在外交实践中，声明一般是由政府或政府部门发表的。但是有些有影响的领袖人物有时也发表个人声明（斯大林、毛泽东生前有时发表个人声明；美国的总统和国务卿也常发表个人声明。国家领导人举行记者招待会或发表对外谈话实际上也都是个人声明）。但考虑到实用性的问题，本单元主要涉及的是政府或政府部门发表的声明。

Contents and Features

A government statement can be issued at different levels according to its weight. In the case of China, we may find statements of the government of the People's Republic of China, statements of the Ministry of Foreign Affairs, statements by the spokesman for the Ministry of Foreign Affairs and statements by the spokesman for the Information Department of the Ministry of Foreign Affairs.

The statements mentioned above are unilateral statements issued in the name of one country. Like diplomatic speeches, they also constitute an important means for a government to make promptly known its feelings, reactions, stand and policies on current major international issues or on issues directly involving its national interests. A government can issue statements whenever it deems necessary and appropriate. Statements made by the spokesmen of the Foreign Ministry during regular press briefings are in fact government statements.

There are also bilateral, sometimes even multilateral statements which are usually issued at the end of official visits or international conferences. They are, in such cases, joint statements or joint declarations.

（二）内容和特点

1. 声明的类别

（1）按发表主体个数的不同，外交声明分为一国声明和联合声明。所谓一国声明（unilateral statement），即一个国家或其领导人，就国际问题或事件表明立场、观点、态度和主张的、公开发表的外交声明。

（李啸尘，2001）

所谓联合声明（joint statement），即两个或两个以上国家或其领导人，对国际上的某一问题或事件，因所持立场、观点和主张相同，而共同公开发表的外交声明。

（2）也可以按发表主体不同进行分类。首先是以外交部名义发表的声明，它可以根据需要添加一些事实材料作为其附件；其次是新闻单位奉命发表的声明，这种形式的声明既是一种新闻消息的发布，又是代表政府对某些问题所做的表态；再次是以国家的一定单位（如外交部新闻司）或个人（如外交部发言人或有影响的领袖人物）用发表谈话的形式发表的声明，这种声明一般语调较客气、涉及的问题较具体，其郑重性次于新闻单位奉命发表的声明。

2. 声明的特点

（1）公开宣布性。因为声明的目的是要发表自己的立场、观点、态度和主张，所以就必须要求它是要公开宣布的。

（2）迅速及时性。某一事情发生之后一定要在第一时间表明自己的态度和立场，因此声明就具有了迅速及时性的特点。

（3）旗帜鲜明性。是指发表声明时一定要旗帜鲜明地明确自己的态度，不能模棱两可。

（李啸尘，2001）

Writing Requirement

Statement is very formal and solemn. Therefore, the writing of statement must be treated seriously and carefully in order to show the stand, viewpoint and attitude clearly. The language of it should be accurate, simple and powerful. The structure of it can be divided into three parts: title, body and signature.

（三）写作要求

由于外交声明具有庄严、郑重的性质，因此在撰写时必须以认真和慎重的态度来对待。在外交声明中要表明的立场、观点、态度，而且主张的部分必须写得旗帜鲜明、清楚明白。其语言应力求准确、庄重、简洁、有力。具体来讲，有以下几点要求：

（1）行文必须周到、严密。凡是文中涉及的问题，都要交代清楚。

（2）多采用条款式结构。这样做是为了达到清楚明晰、使人一目了然的效果。

（3）用语力求简洁、严谨。语言要简练，尽量少说废话；同时，逻辑要严谨，不能胡说、乱说、漏洞百出。

（李啸尘，2001）

具体来说，外交声明通常由标题、正文和落款三部分组成。

（1）标题（title）。标题一般由发表声明的国家、政府、政党的名称、事由组成。标题有两种写法：一种是发表声明的主体加“声明”的字体，如“中华人民共和国政府声明”“中华人民共和国和××共和国政府声明”；另一种是在前一种的基础上加上有关的事由，如“中华人民共和国政府和葡萄牙共和国政府关于澳门问题的联合声明”。

（2）正文（body）。正文部分先要说明发表声明的事由，有的还须对有关事由做具体的陈述，并在此基础上表明发表者对相关问题或事件的立场、观点、态度和主张等。写声明具体内容，用条款式的写法。正文的最后一条往往是正文的结尾，写声明的日期、时间和地点，以及文本的书写语种和效力。

（3）落款（signature）。写声明方的名称，代表姓名（签名）。单发声明通常写明发表的时间，如果时间已在标题下方用括号标出，也可以不用落款部分。联合声明通常在落款处写明发表声明的主体或其代表的签名以及发表声明的时间和地点。

（蔡践，2005）

Case Studies
二、案例分析

（一）国家声明

Statement on the Soviet Military Invasion into Afghanistan
Statement of the Government of the People's Republic of China
December 39, 1979

Recently, the Soviet Union brazenly made a massive military invasion into Afghanistan, grossly interfering in its internal affairs. This armed intervention wantonly violates all norms of international relations. It not only encroaches upon the sovereignty and independence of Afghanistan but poses a grave threat to peace and security in Asia and the whole world. The Chinese Government vigorously condemns this hegemonistic action of the Soviet Union and firmly demands the cessation of this aggression and intervention in Afghanistan and the withdrawal of all Soviet armed forces.

The Soviet Union has long planned for this military invasion of Afghanistan. This is its grave step a southward thrust to the Indian Ocean and the control of sea lanes; it is also an important part of the Soviet strategy for seizing oil-producing areas, outflanking Europe and so gaining world hegemony. The Soviet authorities have never had scruples in trying to realize their hegemonist ambition; but this time they have acted most outrageously. From pulling the strings and using surrogates, their method has escalated to direct involvement with their own troops, armed occupation of a sovereign country and change of its government by violent means. They have extended the use of the "theory of limited sovereignty" from their "community of nations" to a nonaligned and Islamic country of the third world.

It is utterly preposterous for the Soviet Union to invoke the United Nations Charter in defense of its aggression. People remember how the Soviet Union pretentiously proposed the inadmissibility of hegemonism at this very session of the U. N. General Assembly. However, scarcely did the General Assembly adopt a resolution against hegemonism when the Soviet Union, shedding all disguise, launched a naked military aggression wantonly challenging and flouting the United Nations Charter and principles of international law.

The Soviet Union claims that its armed intervention in Afghanistan was undertaken in fulfillment of treaty obligations at the request of the Afghan Government. This sophistry can fool no one. But this aggressor's logic warrants close attention. By its actions the Soviet Union shows that it is prepared to follow this logic and invade and occupy any country it wishes to invade and occupy. The Soviet Union itself acted according to this logic, and Viet Nam, under Soviet instigation, used the same pretext for its armed invasion and occupation of Kampuchea. How could the people of the world fail to be alerted by what is hidden behind the Soviet eagerness to sign "treaties of friendship and cooperation"?

The current Soviet armed aggression in Afghanistan is a big show of Soviet hegemonism. People have come to see more clearly the source of the main threat to world peace and the true nature of this so-called "natural ally" of the third world. They have also come to see more clearly the Soviet hegemonists are most truculent and adventuristic, that the Soviet aggressive ambitions are unlimited, and that Soviet acts of aggression must be stopped effectively. The perverted Soviet action has already aroused the Afghan people to resistance and caused the grave concern of all countries and met with their strong condemnation. The Chinese Government and people will work tirelessly with all countries and people who love peace and uphold justice to frustrate Soviet acts of aggression and expansion.

（文献来源：黄金祺编：《英汉对照外交文献文书教程》（上册），世界知识出版社2004年版，第490－492页。）

Analysis

As title shows, the unilateral statement is about the position of Chinese government on Soviet Union's aggression in Afghanistan. It indicates Chinese government's stark protest towards Soviet Union's aggression. This statement does not include signature which has been made clear in title.

（二）联合声明

中华人民共和国和大不列颠及北爱尔兰联合王国政府关于香港问题的联合声明

中华人民共和国政府和大不列颠及北爱尔兰联合王国政府满意地回顾了近年来两国政府和两国人民之间的友好关系，一致认为通过协商妥善地解决历史上遗留下来的香港问题，有助于维持香港的繁荣与稳定，并有助于两国关系在新的基础上进一步巩固和发展，为此，经过两国政府代表团的会谈，同意声明如下：

一、中华人民共和国政府声明：收回香港地区（包括香港岛、九龙和“新界”，以下称香港）是全中国人民的共同愿望，中华人民共和国政府决定于一九九七年七月一日对香港恢复行使主权。

二、联合王国政府声明：联合王国政府于一九九七年七月一日将香港交还给中华人民共和国。

三、中华人民共和国政府声明，中华人民共和国对香港的基本方针政策如下：

（一）为了维护国家的统一和领土完整，并考虑到香港的历史和现实情况，中华人民共和国决定在对香港恢复行使主权时，根据中华人民共和国宪法第三十一条的规定，设立香港特别行政区。

（二）香港特别行政区直辖于中华人民共和国中央人民政府。除外交和国防事务属中央人民政府管理外，香港特别行政区享有高度的自治权。

（三）香港特别行政区享有行政管理权、立法权、独立的司法权和终审权。现行的法律基本不变。

（四）香港特别行政区政府由当地人组成。行政长官在当地通过选举或协商产生，由中央人民政府任命。主要官员由香港特别行政区行政长官提名，报中央人民政府任命。原在香港各政府部门任职的中外籍公务、警务人员可以留用。香港特别行政区各政府部门可以聘请英籍人士或其他外籍人士担任顾问或某些公职。

（五）香港的现行社会、经济制度不变，生活方式不变。香港特别行政区依法保障人身、言论、出版、集会、结社、旅行、迁徙、通信、罢工、选择职业和学术研究以及宗教信仰等各项权利和自由。私人财产、企业所有权、合法继承权以及外来投资均受法律保护。

（六）香港特别行政区将保持自由港和独立关税地区的地位。

（七）香港特别行政区将保持国际金融中心的地位，继续开放外汇、黄金、证券、期货等市场，资金进出自由。港币继续流通，自由兑换。

（八）香港特别行政区将保持财政独立。中央人民政府不向香港特别行政区征税。

（九）香港特别行政区可同联合王国和其他国家建立互利的经济关系。联合王国和其他国家在香港的经济利益将得到照顾。

（十）香港特别行政区可以“中国香港”的名义单独地同各国、各地区及有关国际组织保持和发展经济、文化关系，并签订有关协定。香港特别行政区政府可自行签发出入香港的旅行证件。

（十一）香港特别行政区的社会治安由香港特别行政区政府负责维持。

（十二）关于中华人民共和国对香港的上述基本方针政策和本联合声明附件一对上述基本方针政策的具体说明，中华人民共和国全国人民代表大会将以中华人民共和国香港特别行政区基本法规定之，并在五十年内不变。

四、中华人民共和国政府和联合王国政府声明：自本联合声明生效之日起至一九九七年六月三十日止的过渡时期内，联合王国政府负责香港的行政管理，以维护和保持香港的经济繁荣和社会稳定；对此，中华人民共和国政府将给予合作。

五、中华人民共和国政府和联合王国政府声明：为求本联合声明得以有效执行，并保证一九九七年政权的顺利交接，在本联合声明生效时成立中英联合联络小组；联合联络小组将根据本联合声明附件二的规定建立和履行职责。

六、中华人民共和国政府和联合王国政府声明：关于香港土地契约和其他有关事项，将根据本联合声明附件三的规定处理。

七、中华人民共和国政府和联合王国政府同意，上述各项声明和本联合声明的附件均将付诸实施。

八、本联合声明须经批准，并自互换批准书之日起生效。批准书应于一九八五年六月三十日前在北京互换。本联合声明及其附件具有同等约束力。

一九八四年十二月十九日在北京签订，共两份，每份都用中文和英文写成，两种文本具有同等效力。

（文献来源：张爽：《英国政治经济与外交》，知识产权出版社 2014 年版，第 243 页。）

分析概要

这份声明是中英两国政府就香港问题发表的，很明显是一份联合声明。它完整地展示了联合声明对于格式、结构和内容的要求。声明由三部分构成——题目、正文和落款。题目是以国家名称和有关的问题来命名的；正文以条款的方式来呈现，用词严谨，语言风格正式；落款是两国代表的签名。

Supplementary Reading
三、拓展阅读

阅读下面两则声明，思考问题。

Statement on the Middle East Peace Process, European Political Cooperation 10 October 1991

The Community and its member States reaffirm their full support for the Middle East peace initiative promoted by the United States and the USSR. They welcome the agreement in principle of all the parties to the dispute to the approach proposed by the US Secretary of State Mr. Baker. In this respect they also welcome the positive attitude of the Palestine National Council. They hope that this emerging consensus will open the way to an early resolution of the problem of an authentic Palestinian representation. They do not believe that any formula on this issue can be held to prejudice negotiations on substantive issues such as the status of Jerusalem.

The Community and its member States continue to attach importance to the adoption by both sides of confidence-building measures designed to create the right climate for successful negotiations. They underline the importance they attach to a suspension of Israeli settlement activity in the Occupied Territories including East Jerusalem, and welcome the willingness of Arab States to freeze the trade boycott of Israel in return for this.

They reaffirm their strong disapproval of the "Zionism is Racism" Resolution passed by the United Nations General Assembly which they believe should be consigned to oblivion.

While reaffirming their well-known positions of principle, the Community andits member States confirm their determination to give all possible support to efforts to convene a Middle East Peace Conference and their determination to play an active role as a full participant in such a Conference alongside the co-sponsors.

They believe that an unprecedented opportunity to create peace between Israel and the Arabs now exists and they call on all parties to show the flexibility and imagination necessary to grasp this.

（文献来源：Christopher Hill & Karen E. Smith, *European Foreign Policy—Key Documents*, London: Routledge, 2000, pp. 308 – 309.）

Reading Comprehension

Directions: Please give brief answers to the following questions.

1. This is a statement issued by European Community and its member states. Except for nation state, are there any other actors who can make a statement?
2. What's the purpose of this statement?

中华人民共和国政府就中华人民共和国同美利坚合众国建立外交关系于 1978 年 12 月 16 日发表的声明

中华人民共和国和美利坚合众国自 1979 年 1 月 1 日起互相承认并建立外交关系，从而结束了长期不正常状态。这是中美两国关系中的历史性事件。

众所周知，中华人民共和国政府是中国的唯一合法政府，台湾是中国的一部分。台湾问题曾经是阻碍中美两国实现关系正常化的关键问题。根据上海公报的精神，经过中美双方的共同努力，现在这个问题在中美两国之间得到了解决，从而使中美两国人民热切的关系得以实现。至于解决台湾回归祖国、完成国家统一的方式，这完全是中国的内政。

为促进中美两国人民的友谊和两国良好关系的进一步发展，应美国政府的邀请，中华人民共和国国务院副总理邓小平将于 1979 年 1 月份对美国进行正式访问。

（文献来源：刘海藩、白占群：《历史的丰碑：中华人民共和国国史全鉴——（八）外交卷》，中共中央文献出版社 2005 年版，第 335 页。）

Reading Comprehension

Directions: Please give brief answers to the following questions.

1. 该声明发表的背景是什么？有什么意义？
2. 该声明的主要内容有哪些？
3. 相比其他声明，该声明在格式上有什么不同点？

5.2 Communiqué
第二节 公报

Basic knowledge
一、基础知识

Introduction

A communiqué is also a kind of statements, but it is usually bilateral or multilateral. So it is mostly in the form of a joint communiqué. Sometimes it may be called a joint press communiqué, which is less formal than a joint communiqué.

Communiqués record or reflect agreements that are reached or commitments that are respectively undertaken by two or more governments on bilateral or multilateral problems, or stand and policies they have decided to jointly adopt on major international issues of common interest.

Nearly all communiqués concern important political affairs and carry a certain weight in international relations. Many of them are of historic significance. Like speeches, communiqués have no rigid forms either. Of course, there are also some general rules to follow in drafting them.

Besides, joint statements (declarations) or joint communiqué can also be used as a form of treaty instruments with binding force.

（一）简介

外交公报是国家、政府、政党、团体向国内外公布重大事件或重要会议情况与决议的正式报道。联合公报是其主要形式。它是关于谈判或会议经过、进展情况，或就某些问题达成协议的正式公文，通常称“联合新闻公报”或“联合公报”，公报主要反映多国政府就双边或多边问题所达成的协议或各自应承担的义务，或他们就共同关心的重大国际问题所决定联合采取的立场和政策，有时也可用作一种有条约约束力的协议文件形式。

（方贤华，1993）

Contents and Features

According to the number of issuing countries, there are two kinds of communiqué: unilateral communiqué and multilateral communiqué. In addition, we can divide communiqué into different categories by its content or purpose.

The features of communiqué can be summarized as formal, succinct and accurate. Some communiqué specifies the rights and obligations of state or government on important political issues; therefore, they can be recognized as the treaty.

（二）内容和特点

1. 公报的类别

根据发表主体个数的不同，外交公报分为单发公报和联发公报。

单发公报主要用于以一国或其政府的名义，正式向外报道关于国家领导人出访、来访的消息等。

联发公报通常称为联合公报，是两个或两个以上国家、政府、政党、团体所共同发表的关于国际重大问题、事件的会谈进展情况、经过、达成的协议的正式文件，用以表明双方或多方的共同看法；或作为对会议情况的正式报道；或作为经过谈判达成的具有承担一定权利与义务的协议文书。其中政治性、新闻报道性联合公报报道对国际重大问题的讨论情况，多无实质性内容，属于对礼节性友好往来的正式报道。它不需要双方代表签署，仅由双方议定文稿，在各自首都的重要报刊上发表。而条约性联合公报反映双方或多方对共同关心的事件经过谈判达成的协议，规定各方承担的权利与义务等，须经各自全权代表签署，以昭信守。

2. 公报的特点

（1）内容重要而又公开，对象广泛而又不确定，文字简练准确而又通俗。

（2）有些联合公报规定了国家和政府的权利和义务等重大政治问题，因此具有条约性质。

（李啸尘，2001）

Writing Requirement

The writing of communiqué must be concise and precise. Generally, it consists of title, body and signature. Clauses are the most important part of communiqué, and should be considered carefully without any part omitted. Besides, the words and expressions should be accurate.

（三）写作要求

（1）条款齐备。条款是公报的主要内容，必须要考虑周全、无一遗漏。

（2）表达准确。文字表达要做到准确无误，确定无疑，如果条款齐备了，但文字表达不准确，可以这样解释，也可以那样解释，或因标点书写造成数字差错、意思改变，会产生不良后果。

公报没有严格的格式，它的撰写要求文字简洁、准确，一般由标题、正文、落款三部分组成。

（1）标题（title）。标题由国民或政府名、事由和文种（如联合公报）组成，如《中华人民共和国和吉布提共和国关于建立外交关系的联合公报》。

（2）正文（body）。正文是公报的内容。如建交联合公报，正文开头写"××国政府与××国政府决定自××××年×月×日起建立大使级外交关系并互派大使"，接着写两国政府共同的外交原则和共同愿意，然后再分别写对方的承诺，最后写发展友好合作关系的信心等。

（3）落款（signature）。落款写国家、政府的代表职衔、姓名（签字）以及日期。

（李啸尘，2001）

Case Studies

二、案例分析

（一）联合公报

Joint Communiqué between the People's Republic of China and the United States of America

August 17, 1982

（1）In the Joint Communiqué on the Establishment of Diplomatic Relations on January 1, 1979, issued by the Government of the United States of America and the Government of the People's Republic of China, the United States of America recognized the Government of the People's Republic of China as the sole legal Government of China, and it acknowledged the Chinese position that there is but one China and Taiwan is part of China. Within that context, the two sides agreed that the people of the United States would continue to maintain cultural, commercial, and other unofficial relations with the people of Taiwan. On this basis, relations between the United States and China were normalized.

(2) The question of United States arms sales to Taiwan was not settled in the course of negotiations between the two countries on establishing diplomatic relations. The two sides held differing positions, and the Chinese side stated that it would raise the issue again following normalization. Recognizing that this issue would seriously hamper the development of United States-China relations, they have held further discussions on it, during and since the meetings between President Ronald Reagan and Premier Zhao Ziyang and between Secretary of State Alexander M. Haig, Jr. and Vice Premier and Foreign Minister Huang Hua in October 1981.

(3) Respect for each other's sovereignty and territorial integrity and non-interference in each other's internal affairs constitute the fundamental principles guiding United States-China relations. These principles were confirmed in the Shanghai Communiqué of February 28, 1972 and reaffirmed in the Joint Communiqué on the Establishment of Diplomatic Relations which came into effect on January 1, 1979. Both sides emphatically state that these principles continue to govern all aspects of their relations.

(4) The Chinese Government reiterates that the question of Taiwan is China's internal affair. The message to Compatriots in Taiwan issued by China on January 1, 1979 promulgated a fundamental policy of striving for peaceful reunification of the motherland. The Nine-Point Proposal put forward by China on September 30, 1981 represented a further major effort under this fundamental policy to strive for a peaceful solution to the Taiwan question.

(5) The United States Government attaches great importance to its relations with China, and reiterates that it has no intention of infringing on Chinese sovereignty and territorial integrity, or interfering in China's internal affairs, or pursuing a policy of "two Chinas" or "one China, one Taiwan". The United States Government understands and appreciates the Chinese policy of striving for a peaceful resolution of the Taiwan question as indicated in China's

Message to Compatriots in Taiwan issued on January 1, 1979 and the Nine-Point Proposal put forward by China on September 30, 1981. The new situation which has emerged with regard to the Taiwan question also provides favorable conditions for the settlement of United States-China differences over United States arms sales to Taiwan.

(6) Having in mind the foregoing statements of both sides, the United States Government states that it does not seek to carry out a long-term policy of arms sales to Taiwan, that its arms sales to Taiwan will not exceed, either in qualitative or in quantitative terms, the level of those supplied in recent years since the establishment of diplomatic relations between the United States and China, and that it intends gradually to reduce its sale of arms to Taiwan, leading, over a period of time, to a final resolution. In so stating, the United States acknowledges China's consistent position regarding the thorough settlement of this issue.

(7) In order to bring about, over a period of time, a final settlement of the question of United States arms sales to Taiwan, which is an issue rooted in history, the two Governments will make every effort to adopt measures and create conditions conducive to the thorough settlement of this issue.

(8) The development of United states-China relations is not only in the interests of the two peoples but also conducive to peace and stability in the world. The two sides are determined, on the principle of equality and mutual benefit, to strengthen their ties in the economic, cultural, educational, scientific, technological and other fields and make strong, joint efforts for the continued development of relations between the Governments and peoples of the United States and China.

(9) In order to bring about the healthy development of United States-China relations, maintain world peace and oppose aggression and expansion, the two Governments reaffirm the principles agreed on by the two sides in the Shanghai Communiqué and the Joint Communiqué on the Establishment of Diplomatic Relations. The two sides will maintain contact and hold appropriate consultations on bilateral and international issues of common

interest.

（文献来源：新华网，http: //news. xinhuanet. com，检索日期：2015 年 2 月 16 日。）

Analysis

The three Sino-US communiqués are a collection of three joint statements made by the governments of the United States and the People's Republic of China, including Shanghai communiqué, Joint communiqué on the Establishment of Diplomatic Relations and August 17 communiqué. This is August 17 communiqué that reaffirms the desire of both sides to further strengthen economic, cultural, educational, scientific, and technological ties. Both sides also reaffirmed the statements made about the Taiwan issue in the previous communiqué. Although no definitive conclusions were reached on the issue of arms sale to Taiwan, the United States did declare its intent to gradually decrease its sale of arms to Taiwan.

（二）单发公报

关于中华人民共和国主席江泽民访问俄罗斯联邦并与叶利钦总统举行非正式会晤的联合新闻公报

1998 年 11 月

应俄罗斯联邦总统鲍·尼·叶利钦的邀请，中华人民共和国主席江泽民于 1998 年 11 月 22 日至 25 日对俄罗斯进行访问。

两国元首于 11 月 23 日成功地举行了首次非正式会晤。这次会晤表明，通过两国领导人之间的定期接触，双方相互理解与信任达到了崭新的水平。

中华人民共和国主席江泽民还会见了俄罗斯联邦总理叶·马·普里

马科夫、俄罗斯联邦会议联邦委员会主席叶·谢·斯特罗耶夫和俄罗斯联邦会议国家杜马主席根·尼·谢列兹尼奥夫。双方就会晤成果发表了联合声明，强调指出，双方在中俄第六次最高级会晤期间就世纪之交国际社会发展的基本趋势协调了立场，并就进一步加强双边合作的长期战略前景达成共识。

江泽民和叶利钦满意地指出，中俄关系正沿着1996年建立的平等信任、面向21世纪的战略协作伙伴关系的轨道稳步发展，强调双方做出这一选择既是根据对双边关系历史经验和当今世界现实的思考，也是基于对两国合作前景和国际形势发展所达成的共识。两国元首确认，根据1994年9月3日签署的中俄国界西段协定进行的中俄国界西段勘界工作的所有野外作业已全部按期完成。中俄国界东、西两段已勘定的边界在两国关系史上首次在实地得到明确标示。两国在亚洲大陆创立了新型的边境安全模式，即不仅要划定边界线，而且要在边境地区裁减军事力量，建立信任措施和增加军事透明度。双方通过会谈就双边关系的具体问题达成了一系列重要协议。

双方一致认为，必须采取协调一致的重大步骤，加强对中俄经贸合作的组织管理，改善其金融和法律条件。责成中俄总理定期会晤委员会及各分委会于今年底或明年初召开例会，研究双方各具体领域合作中存在的问题，并将共同研究的结果和建议提交定于1999年春天在莫斯科举行的第四次总理定期会晤审议。中方同意俄方关于尽快就两国公民往来问题举行商谈的建议。

双方商定，于近期对俄罗斯联邦驻北京使馆和驻上海总领馆，以及中华人民共和国驻莫斯科使馆的现有外交房产进行登记。中华人民共和国获得其驻圣彼得堡总领馆建筑的产权后，俄方将为其登记提供必要协助。双方还将就两国在对方境内的其他外交房产问题加紧进行谈判。俄方重申在台湾问题上的一贯立场，即中华人民共和国政府是中国的唯一合法政府，台湾是中国领土不可分割的一部分。基于这一原则立场，俄方不支持任何形式的关于“台湾独立”的构想，据此，俄方支持中华人民共和国关于不接受“两个中国”“一中一台”的立场，反对接纳台湾加入联合国及其他只能由主权国家参加的国际组织，重申不向台湾出售武器。中方对俄方在台湾问题上一贯坚持一个中国的原则表示衷心感谢，对俄罗斯在经贸、科技、文化、体育等领域与台湾进行非官方联系不持异议。

中方重申，完全支持俄罗斯联邦的统一和领土完整。

两国领导人还就国际局势及进一步加强中俄在国际事务中的合作问题深入交换了意见。双方重申，在巴尔干、波斯湾及亚太地区局势、亚洲金融危机后果、南亚局势、联合国安理会改革及其他迫切的国际问题上，中俄立场一致或相近。双方商定，将就迫切的国际问题加强磋商，协调立场。双方还商定，要完善各个级别，首先是高层对话机制，为此将充分利用北京—莫斯科直通保密电话就重要问题交换意见。

江泽民主席邀请鲍·尼·叶利钦总统于 1999 年访华，举行第七次最高级会晤。叶利钦总统接受邀请并表示感谢，具体日期将通过外交途径商定。

（文献来源：李啸尘主编：《办公室工作标准运作典范全书·公文写作秘书卷》，中国言实出版社 2001 年版，第 522－523 页。）

分析概要

这是 1998 年江泽民访问俄罗斯时中国政府发表的公报，是一篇单发公报。公报包含了江主席当时出访时与俄总统商谈的话题、内容以及行程路线图等，表明了双方在一些重大问题上的立场和主张。

该篇公报没有以条款的方式，而是以段落的方式来呈现的，充分表明公报的格式是灵活多样的，只要把问题说清楚，具体写作要求也可以灵活调整。

Supplementary Readings
三、拓展阅读

阅读下面的公报，回答问题。

Joint Communiqué between China and Portugal

JOINT COMMUNIQUE OF THE GOVERNMENT OF THE PEOPLE'S REPUBLIC OF CHINA AND THE REPUBLIC OF PORTUGAL ON THE ESTABLISHMENT OF DIPLOMATIC RELATIONS BETWEEN CHINA AND PORTUGAL

The People's Republic of China and the government of the Republic of Portugal have decided to establish diplomatic relations at ambassadorial level as from February 8, 1979 and to exchange ambassadors within three months.

The two governments will maintain their diplomatic relations in conformity with principles of mutual respect for sovereignty and territorial integrity, non-interference in each other's internal affairs, and equality and mutual benefit.

The Government of the Republic of Portugal recognizes that the Government of The People's Republic of China is the sole legal government of China, and that Taiwan is an inalienable part of the People's Republic of China. The Government of Portugal states that its diplomatic relations with Taiwan were already severed back in January 1975.

The Government of China and Portugal have agreed mutually to provide all necessary assistance for the establishment and performance of the functions of diplomatic missions in their respective capitals on the basis of equality and mutual benefit and accordance with international practice.

(Signed)
Han Kehuan
Ambassador Extraordinary and
Plenipotentiary of the People's
Republic of China to the Republic
of France

(Signed)
Antonio Coimbra Martins
Ambassador Extraordinary and
Plenipotentiary of the Republic of
Portugal to the Republic of
France
Paris, February 8, 1979

（文献来源：黄金祺编：《英汉对照外交文献文书教程》（上册），世界知识出版社 2004 年版，第 570－571 页。）

Reading Comprehension

Directions: Please give brief answers to the following questions.

1. What's the major difference between this Communiqué and other kinds of Communiqué?
2. What's the main content of the Communiqué?

加强互联互通伙伴关系对话会联合新闻公报
（2014 年 11 月 8 日，北京）

我们，中华人民共和国主席习近平、孟加拉人民共和国总统哈米德、柬埔寨王国首相洪森、老挝人民民主共和国主席朱马里、蒙古国总统额勒贝格道尔吉、缅甸联邦总统吴登盛、巴基斯坦伊斯兰共和国总理谢里夫、塔吉克斯坦共和国总统拉赫蒙，于 2014 年 11 月 8 日在北京举行加强互联互通伙伴关系对话会。会议由中华人民共和国主席习近平主持。联合国亚太经社会执行秘书阿赫塔尔、上海合作组织秘书长梅津采夫参加会议。

我们认为，经济建设和改善民生是亚洲各国的优先任务，深化亚洲各国经济合作与和平发展、推进区域一体化是亚洲人民的共同意志。当前，国际金融危机影响犹存，外部需求不足，对资本、市场和技术的竞争日趋激烈，亚洲国家面临不进则退的压力。在此形势下，互联互通有利于寻找新增长点和培育新竞争优势，是亚洲合作与持续繁荣的新动力。

我们赞赏地注意到，亚太经合组织第二十二次领导人非正式会议将于 2014 年 11 月 10 日至 11 日在北京举行，并将讨论全方位基础设施与互联互通建设问题。我们期待会议制定亚太经合组织互联互通蓝图，支持亚太经合组织继续致力于本地区互联互通并做出新的贡献。

我们认为，互联互通是时代潮流，也是亚洲国家的共同需要，应覆盖亚洲所有国家，使本地区所有国家和人民公平受益。只有各国政府、国际和区域组织、私营部门和广大民众共同参与，亚洲才能实现全方位、高水平的互联互通。

我们指出，发展中国家特别是内陆国家在互联互通方面面临运输和贸易成本高以及资金、技术、自然条件等多方面制约，国际社会包括过境国应充分考虑上述国家的特殊需要和困难，加大支持力度。

我们认为，21 世纪亚洲互联互通是“三位一体”的联通，包括交通基础设施的硬件联通，规章制度、标准、政策的软件联通，以及增进民间友好互信和文化交流的人文联通，涵盖政策沟通、设施联通、贸易畅通、资金融通和民心相通五大领域。基础设施建设是互联互通的基础和优先。

我们认为，互联互通是亚洲各国的共同事业，当前既面临难得的历史机遇，也存在不少挑战。我们决心加强互联互通伙伴关系，深化务实合作，谋求共同发展：

——加大交通等基础设施建设力度，实现亚洲国家的联动发展。我们认为，亚洲各国发展战略和基建规划对接，可以发挥比较优势和后发优势，在全球供应链、产业链和价值链中占据有利位置，提高综合竞争力，实现强劲、可持续、平衡增长。我们可以通过加强物流和交通运输基础设施合作，促进地区货物和商品过境运输，扩大地区生产网络，深化区域经济合作。

——坚持开放的区域主义，塑造开放的亚洲经济格局。我们鼓励域内外国家加强合作，各尽其能，优势互补，利益共享，不搞封闭性集团，不针对第三国。当务之急是协商解决影响互联互通的制度和标准问题，切实降低人员、商品、资金跨境流动的成本与时间。在此过程中，应尊重各国主权和领土完整，照顾各方舒适度，不强人所难，不干涉他国内政。

——坚持以人为本和发展导向，实现亚洲人民繁荣和幸福的梦想。我们认为，互联互通应与亚洲国家政治、经济、社会、文化、生态等重大发展战略相结合，产业升级、创造就业和消除贫困并行推进，特别重视帮助基层民众摆脱贫困，增加收入，解决用电、饮水、医疗、教育等现实问题，提高亚洲各国人民的幸福指数。

——完善体制和机制，打造亚洲特色的合作平台。我们赞赏亚太经合组织、联合国亚太经社会、上海合作组织、东南亚国家联盟、南亚区域合作联盟、经济合作组织、世界银行、亚洲开发银行等有关国际和区域组织为促进亚洲互联互通开展的工作和取得的成果。希望各机制分工协作，优势互补，形成合力。我们将继续保持政府间沟通协调，同时动员各方面力量，建立私营部门、智库和学术机构等广泛参与的合作网络。

我们支持着力解决基础设施互联互通的资金瓶颈问题，创新融资机制。作为对世界银行、亚洲开发银行等现有金融机构的有益补充，我们支持中国等有关国家共同成立亚洲基础设施投资银行。

我们支持“丝绸之路经济带”和“21 世纪海上丝绸之路”（“一带一路”）倡议。该倡议深受历史启迪又有鲜明时代特色，与亚洲互联互通建设相辅相成，将为沿线国家增进政治互信、深化经济合作和密切民间往来及文化交流注入强大动力，具有巨大合作潜力和广阔发展前景。我们欢迎并赞赏中国宣布成立丝路基金，为亚洲国家参与互联互通合作提供投融资支持。

我们致力于共商、共建、共享“一带一路”。“一带一路”源于亚洲，应以亚洲国家为重点方向，优先关注和实现亚洲的互联互通；以陆路经济走廊和海上经济合作为依托，建立亚洲互联互通基本框架；以交通基础设施为突破，实现亚洲互联互通早期收获；以人文交流为纽带，夯实亚洲互联互通的社会根基。

我们注意到蒙古国提出的“草原之路”倡议，相信这一倡议将对加强欧亚互联互通发挥积极作用。

我们支持联合国亚太经社会发展基于亚洲高速公路和泛亚铁路网络的一体化协同联运系统，这将有助于区域互联互通的可持续性。我们也支持联合国亚太经社会提出的亚太信息高速公路倡议，该倡议旨在联接各国的主干网络并将其整合为陆海一体的光纤基础设施。

我们认为，世界已迈入经济全球化、政治多极化、文化多样化和社会信息化时代，所有国家既独立自主又命运攸关，相互依存。互联互通伙伴关系是亚洲各国伙伴关系的重要组成部分，也是亚洲发展和命运共同体建设的应有之义。我们呼吁亚洲各国加强合作，不断提高亚洲互联互通水平，为实现亚洲持久发展和繁荣而共同努力。

（文献来源：中华人民共和国外交部网站，http://www.fmprc.gov.cn/web/ziliao_674904/1179_674909/t1208704.shtml，检索日期：2015年12月12日。）

Reading Comprehension

Directions: Please give brief answers to the following questions.

1. 该公报由几部分组成？
2. 在格式上，该公报有什么独特之处？
3. 该公报传达了什么战略？

5.3 Exercises
课后练习

- **True or False**

Directions: Read the following sentences and decide whether they are true or false.

1. Statement is one kind of document of declarations.
2. In diplomatic practice, a statement is generally issued by a government.
3. A government statement can only be issued at state level.
4. A communiqué is also a kind of statements.
5. Statements and communiqué have no rigid forms.

- **Gap-filling**

Directions: Complete each sentence with appropriate words.

1. Statements made by the ________ during regular press briefings are in fact government statements.
2. The purpose of statement is expressing ________, ________, showing ________, ________ or ________ torelated questions or events.
3. A communiqué is usually ________ or ________, and so is mostly in the form of a joint communiqué.

• Multiple Choices

Directions: In this part there are several incomplete sentences. For each sentence there are four choices marked A, B, C and D. Choose the ONE answer that best completes the sentence.

1. A statement is generally issued by a ________ .
   A. government
   B. groups or foreign institute
   C. media or their president
   D. representatives for an international issue or event
2. Many of communiqués are ________ .
   A. permanent B. historic
   C. temporary D. lasting
3. Joint statements (declarations) or joint communiqué can also be used as a form of treaty instruments having ________ character.
   A. binding B. nonbinding
   C. lawful D. principled

• Translation

Directions: translate the following sentences into the target language.

English-Chinese translation

1. The Chinese Government and people will work tirelessly with all countries and people who love peace and uphold justice to frustrate

Soviet acts of aggression and expansion.

2. The Chinese Government has on many occasions solemnly stated that the continental shelf is the natural prolongation of the land territory.
3. Respect for each other's sovereignty and territorial integrity and Non-interference in each other's internal affairs constitute the fundamental principles guiding United States-China relations.
4. In order to bring about, over a period of time, a final settlement of the question of United States arms sales to Taiwan, which is an issue rooted in history, the two Government will make every effort to adopt measures and create conditions conducive to the thorough settlement of this issue.
5. In order to bring about the healthy development of United States-China relations, maintain world peace and oppose aggression and expansion, the two Governments reaffirm the principles agreed on by the two sides in the Shanghai Communiqué and the Joint Communiqué on the Establishment of Diplomatic Relations.

Chinese-English translation

1. 双方将就共同关心的双边问题和国际问题保持接触并进行适当的磋商。

2. 双方强调声明，这些原则仍是指导双方关系所有方面的原则。

3. 在中华人民共和国政府和美利坚合众国政府发表的一九七九年一月一日建立外交关系的联合公报中，美利坚合众国承认中华人民共和国政府是中国的唯一合法政府，并承认中国的立场，即只有一个中国，台湾是中国的一部分。

4. 中葡两国政府商定，在平等互利的基础上，根据国际惯例，在各自首都为对方的建馆及其执行任务提供一切必要的协助。

5. 两国同意在互相尊重领土和主权完整、互不侵犯、互不干涉内政、平等互利和和平共处五项原则的基础上发展两国之间的友好和合作关系。

• Simulative Exercise

According to what you've learned above, write a statement about the Diaoyu islands on China's position.

6 Documents for Stipulations and Agreements

第六章 规约文书

Abstract

Documents for stipulations and agreements, covering a variety of matters, are widely used. Meanwhile, they have overlapping areas in nature. Documents for stipulations and agreements include laws and regulations, conventions, etc. They differ in the level of restraining force and term of validity.

According to areas of application and objectives, documents for stipulations and agreements fall into two categories: treaty and regulation. The two types of documents will be introduced in terms of their definition, functions and contents. The selected bilingual case studies aim to enhance the understanding of the two documents and to promote the writing skills through practices.

内容概览

规约文书的范围广泛，跨度极大，不同种类的规约文书在性质上互有交叉。规约文书包括法律、法规、章程、公约一类的文书。规约文书具有不同程度的约束力，有效的期限也不相同。

依照不同的应用领域和目的，规约文书可分为条例、条约。本章详细介绍两种规约文书的定义、作用和内容，明确其使用场合及目的。本章以精选的双语案例作为范本，从正反两方面加强读者对两种文书的理解，并通过实战演练提高相关人员关于这两种文书的写作水平。

6.1 Treaty
第一节 条约

Basic Knowledge
一、基础知识

Introduction

A treaty is an agreement entered into by actors in international law, namely sovereign states and international organizations. A treaty may also be known as an (international) agreement, protocol, covenant, convention, pact, or exchange of letters, among other terms. Regardless of terminology, all of these forms of agreements are, under international law, equally considered treaties and the rules are the same.

Treaties can be loosely compared to contracts: both are means of willing parties assuming obligations among themselves, and a party that fails to live up to their obligations can be held liable under international law.

A treaty between two nations is called bilateral treaty; one among three nations or more is called multilateral treaty. A treaty usually comes with a term of validity, and it expires if not extended.

（一）简介

条约是国际法主体之间（两个或若干国家）在政治、经济、军事、文化科技等方面相互权利和义务的协议文件。一般包括公约、协定、换文、联合声明、联合公报、联合宣言、规约、专约等。

（曾富蓉、黄大勇，2002）

由两个国家签订的条约称“双边条约”；三个或三个以上国家签订的条约称“多边条约”。条约一般具有时效性，如果期满不再续签即失效。

Contents and Features

According to its nature, a treaty falls into two categories: lawmaking treaty and contractual treaty.

In terms of how a treaty is implemented, it can be automatic or non-automatic. If a non-automatic treaty is signed, changes may be made to domestic laws according to the treaty.

（一）内容和特点

1. 条约的分类

根据国际法理论，条约可按照参加国数量分为双边条约、多边条约和国际公约三类。双边条约是最常见的、两个国家间缔结的条约；比两国更多的一群国家间缔结的条约通称为多边条约。国际公约也是许多国家参加的，本来可以归入多边条约一类，但因为有些多边条约是在国际会议通过或签订的，有的是由国际组织制定的，对于原来没有参加会议的国家，一般地，或在一定限度内，也是开放的，这类条约特别称为国际公约。

就法律性质而言，条约可分为造法性条约和契约性条约。前者一般缔结于相当多数的国家之间，为他们规定共守的行为规则；契约性条约一般缔结于两个或一小群国家之间，形成彼此间一般关系或特定事项上的一种交易，旨在满足缔约各方不同的目的和不同的利益。

（周鲠生，2009）

2. 条约的特点

（1）条约是以国家的名义出面缔结签订的一种国际性的国家文书。

（2）条约是国际间签订的履行信约的有效方式。

（3）条约是一种国际间书面文字协议文书。

（4）条约一定包含权利和义务的关系。

（方建文、李啸尘，2002）

Writing Requirement

Bilateral treaties should be prepared in duplicate for signing, so that each party can save a copy of the original one after the signing of the treaty.

A treaty should be written in two or multiple languages and stick to the format to avoid misunderstanding.

A treaty signed by heads of states usually includes the following parts: name, title, body and ending.

（二）写作要求

1. 双边条约需准备一式两份以备签署，以便每方都能保存一份经过签署的条约原件。每一国在所保存的原件中享有在先权，即该国文字排在前页或左页，该国国名（或元首和全权代表的姓名）在序言或其他条文中排在前面，该国全权代表或代表的签署在另一国全权代表或代表签署的上方或左方。

2. 当条约是以两种或多种文字写成的，主权平等原则要求条约的两种或多种文本都统一标准。因此，对于各种文本都须十分谨慎，使之尽可能保持一致，以免引起误会。

3. 以国家元首名义缔结的条约一般包括下列部分：

（1）约名（name）。

（2）约首（title）。即序言，包括缔约双方的姓名和职衔；条约宗旨的综述；缔约双方所指派的全权代表的姓名和职衔；叙述“全权代表相互校阅全权证书，认为妥善后议定下列各条”的段落。

（3）约文（body）。即条约的实质性条款。

（4）约尾（ending）。即若干条一般称为“最后条款”的条文，如有关条约的适用范围、签署、批准、加入、生效和有效期的条文。关于批准手续的规定一般需提到交换或存放批准书的地点。有关效期的条文可具体规定条约有效期的年限以及"除非缔约一方在期满前六个月（或一年）书面通知另一方终止条约，条约将继续有效"等内容。

（黄金祺，2004）

Case Studies

二、案例分析

案例一

Treaty on the Non-proliferation of Nuclear Weapons

The States concluding this Treaty, hereinafter referred to as the "Parties to the Treaty".

Considering the devastation that would be visited upon all mankind by a nuclear war and the consequent need to make every effort to avert the danger of such a war and to take measures to safeguard the security of peoples.

Believing that the proliferation of nuclear weapons would seriously enhance the danger of nuclear war.

In conformity with resolutions of the United Nations General Assembly calling for the conclusion of an agreement on the prevention of wider dissemination of nuclear weapons.

Undertaking to co-operate in facilitating the application of International Atomic Energy Agency safeguards on peaceful nuclear activities.

Expressing their support for research, development and other efforts to further the application, within the framework of the International Atomic Energy Agency safeguards system, of the principle of safeguarding effectively the flow of source and special fissionable materials by use of instruments and other techniques at certain strategic points.

Affirming the principle that the benefits of peaceful applications of nuclear technology, including any technological by-products which may be derived by nuclear-weapon States from the development of nuclear explosive devices, should be available for peaceful purposes to all Parties to the Treaty, whether nuclear-weapon or non-nuclear-weapon States.

Convinced that, in furtherance of this principle, all Parties to the Treaty are entitled to participate in the fullest possible exchange of scientific information for, and to contribute alone or in co-operation with other States to, the further development of the applications of atomic energy for peaceful purposes.

Declaring their intention to achieve at the earliest possible date the cessation of the nuclear arms race and to undertake effective measures in the direction of nuclear disarmament.

Urging the co-operation of all States in the attainment of this objective.

Recalling the determination expressed by the Parties to the 1963 Treaty banning nuclear weapon tests in the atmosphere, in outer space and under water in its Preamble to seek to achieve the discontinuance of all test explosions of nuclear weapons for all time and to continue negotiations to this end.

Desiring to further the easing of international tension and the strengthening of trust between States in order to facilitate the cessation of the manufacture of nuclear weapons, the liquidation of all their existing stockpiles, and the elimination from national arsenals of nuclear weapons and the means of their delivery pursuant to a Treaty on general and complete disarmament under strict and effective international control.

Recalling that, in accordance with the Charter of the United Nations, States must refrain in their international relations from the threat or use of force against the territorial integrity orpolitical independence of any State, or in any other manner inconsistent with the Purposes of the United Nations, and that the establishment and maintenance of international peace and security are to be promoted with the least diversion for armaments of the world's human and economicresources.

Have agreed as follows:

Article I

Each nuclear-weapon State Party to the Treaty undertakes not to transfer to any recipient whatsoever nuclear weapons or other nuclear explosive devices or control over such weapons or explosive devices directly, or indirectly; and not in any way to assist, encourage, or induce any non-nuclear-weapon State to manufacture or otherwise acquire nuclear weapons or other nuclear explosive devices, or control over such weapons or explosive devices.

Article II

Each non-nuclear-weapon State Party to the Treaty undertakes not to receive the transfer from any transfer or whatsoever of nuclear weapons or other nuclear explosive devices or of control over such weapons or explosive devices directly, or indirectly; not to manufacture or otherwise acquire nuclear weapons or other nuclear explosive devices; and not to seek or receive any assistance in the manufacture of nuclear weapons or other nuclear explosive devices.

……

Article X

1. Each Party shall in exercising its national sovereignty have the right to withdraw from the Treaty if it decides that extraordinary events, related to the subject matter of this Treaty, have jeopardized the supreme interests of its country. It shall give notice of such withdrawal to allother Parties to the Treaty and to the United Nations Security Council three months in advance. Such notice shall include a statement of the extraordinary events it regards as having jeopardized its supreme interests.

2. Twenty-five years after the entry into force of the Treaty, a conference

shall be convened to decide whether the Treaty shall continue in force indefinitely, or shall be extended for anadditional fixed period or periods. This decision shall be taken by a majority of the Parties to the Treaty.

Article XI

This Treaty, the English, Russian, French, Spanish and Chinese texts of which are equally authentic, shall be deposited in the archives of the Depositary Governments. Duly certified copies of this Treaty shall be transmitted by the Depositary Governments to the Governments ofthe signatory and acceding States.

IN WITNESS WHEREOF the undersigned, duly authorised, have signed this Treaty.

DONE in triplicate, at the cities of London, Moscow and Washington, the first day of July, one thousand nine hundred and sixty-eight.

（文献来源： https: //www. iaea. org/sites/default/files/publications/documents/infcircs/1970/infcirc140. pdf, 检索日期：2016 年 5 月 2 日。）

Analysis

The Treaty on the Non-Proliferation of Nuclear Weapons, commonly known as the Non-Proliferation Treaty or NPT, is an international treaty whose objective is to prevent the spread of nuclear weapons and weapons technology, to promote cooperation in the peaceful uses of nuclear energy, and to further the goal of achieving nuclear disarmament and complete disarmament. In writing of this treaty, much attention has been paid to the format, contents and language proficiency.

案例二

中国尼泊尔边界条约
中华人民共和国和尼泊尔王国边界条约

中华人民共和国主席和尼泊尔国王陛下，

一致认为，正式解决中国和尼泊尔之间的边界问题，符合两国人民的根本利益；

满意地看到，两国间悠久的友好关系，从两国建交以来有了进一步的发展；双方根据和平共处五项原则，本着公平合理和互谅互让的精神，通过友好协商，顺利地、全面地解决了两国边界问题；

坚信两国全部边界的正式划定，并且巩固地成为一条和平友好的边界，不仅是中尼两国友好关系进一步发展的里程碑，而且是对巩固亚洲和世界的和平的贡献；

为此，决定在一九六〇年三月二十一日中华人民共和国政府和尼泊尔国王陛下政府关于两国边界问题的协定的基础上，缔结本条约，并议定下列各条：

第一条

缔约双方以传统习惯边界线为基础，联合进行必要的实地调查和勘察并且根据平等互利、友好互让的原则做出某些调整以后，协议下列从西向东的全部边界线走向，线北为中国领土，线南为尼泊尔领土：

一、中尼边界从卡利河和丁喀河的分水岭与雀河（卡尔那利河）支系为一方、丁喀河为另一方的分水岭的相交处起，界线沿着孔雀河（卡尔那利河）支系为一方、丁喀河和色帖河为另一方的分水岭向东南行，经过纽马吉莎雪山（里普杜腊雪山）山脊和丁喀里普山口（里普杜腊山口），到柏林山口（乌累山口）。

……

十一、从聂鲁桥（牛列桥）起，界线大体向东行，到赤仁玛（高里三喀），沿山脊向东，再沿着绒辖河和绒布河为一方、都得科西河支系为另一方的分水岭向北行，到兰巴山口，再沿山脊大体东南行，经过卓奥友山、普莫里山（尼尔朗古）、珠穆朗玛峰（萨加·玛塔）和洛子峰，到马卡鲁山；然后沿山脊向东南转东而行，到波底山口。

……

第二条

缔约双方同意，凡是以河流为界的地段，以河道中心线为界；如果界河改道，除双方另有协议外，原界线维持不变。

第三条

在本条约签订后，根据一九六〇年三月二十一日双方关于两国边界问题的协定而成立的中尼边界联合委员会，应该在两国的边界线上树立必要的永久性的界桩，然后草拟一项议定书，详细载明整个边界的走向和永久界桩的位置，并且附入标明界线和永久性界桩位置的详图。上述议定书经两国政府签订后，即成为本条约的附件，该项详图将代替本条约目前所附的地图。

在上述议定书签订后，中尼边界联合委员会的任务即告终止，一九六〇年三月二十一日双方关于两国边界问题的协定即行失效。

第四条

缔约双方同意，在两国边界正式划定后，如果发生任何边界争议，应该由双方友好协商解决。

第五条

本条约自签字之日起生效。

本条约于一九六一年十月五日在北京签订，共两份，每份都用中文、尼泊尔文和英文写成，三种文本具有同等效力。

中华人民共和国主席　　　　尼泊尔国王陛下
刘少奇　　　　马亨德拉·比尔·比克拉姆·沙阿·德瓦
（签字）　　　　（签字）

（文献来源：黄金祺编：《英汉对照外交文献文书教程》（下册），世界知识出版社2004年版，第328－330页。）

分析概要

以国家元首名义缔结的条约需要在约首表明缔约双方的姓名和职衔，以及条约宗旨的综述。在约文中要体现条约的实质性条款。在约尾要加入有关条约的适用范围、签署、批准、加入、生效和有效期的条文。

Supplementary Readings
三、拓展阅读

请阅读以下条约并回答问题。

Treaty of Peace and Friendship between the People's Republic of China and Japan

The People's Republic of China and Japan,

Recalling with satisfaction that since the Government of the People's Republic of China and the Government of Japan issued a Joint Statement in Peking on September 29, 1972, the friendly relations between the two Governments and the peoples of the two countries have developed greatly on a new basis,

Confirming that the abovementioned Joint Statement constitutes the basis of the relations of peace and friendship between the two countries and that the principles enunciated in the Joint Statement should be strictly observed,

Confirming that the principles of the Charter of the United Nations should be fully respected,

Hoping to contribute to peace and stability in Asia and in the world,

For the purpose of solidifying and developing the relations of peace and friendship between the two countries,

Have resolved to conclude a Treaty of Peace and Friendship and for that purpose have appointed as their Plenipotentiaries:

The People's Republic of China: Huang Hua,

Minster of Foreign Affairs

Japan: Sunao Sonoda,

Minister for Foreign Affairs

Who are having communicated to each other their full powers, found to be in good and due form, have agreed as follows:

Article I

The Contracting Parties shall develop durable relations of peace and friendship between the two countries on the basis of the principles of mutual respect for sovereignty and territorial integrity, mutual non-aggression, non-interference in each other's internal affairs, equality and mutual benefit and peaceful coexistence.

In keeping with the foregoing principles and the principles of the United Nations Charter, the Contracting Parties affirm that in their mutual relations. All disputes shall be settled by peaceful means without resorting to the use or threat of force.

Article II

The Contracting Parties declare that neither of them should seek hegemony in the Asia-Pacific region or in any other region and that each is opposed to efforts by any other country or group of countries to establish such hegemony.

Article III

The Contracting Parties shall in a good-neighbourly and friendly spirit and in conformity with the principles of equality and mutual benefit and non-interference in each other's internal affairs endeavour to further develop economic and cultural relations between the two countries and to promote exchanges between the peoples of the two countries.

Article IV

The present Treaty shall not affect the position of either Contracting Party regarding its relations with third countries.

Article V

The present Treaty shall be ratified and shall enter into force on the date of the exchange of instruments of ratification which shall take place at Tokyo. The present Treaty shall remain in force for ten years and thereafter shall continue to be in force until terminated in accordance with the provisions of Paragraph 2 of this Article.

Either Contracting Party may, by giving one year's written notice to the other Contracting Party, terminate the present Treaty at the end of the initial ten-year period or at any time thereafter.

In witness whereof the respective Plenipotentiaries have signed the present Treaty and have affixed thereto their seals.

Done in duplicate in the Chinese and Japanese languages, both texts being equally authentic, at Peking, this twelfth day of August 1978.

For the People's Republic of China：
Huang Hua
(Signed)

Note: The two parties exchanged the instruments of ratification on 23 October, 1978 at Tokyo.

（文献来源：黄金祺编：《英汉对照外交文献文书教程》（下册），世界知识出版社2004年版，第331－333页。）

Reading Comprehension

Directions: Please give brief answers to the following questions.

1. What are the source country and target country of the treaty respectively?
2. Can you generalize some basic features of the above treaty?

3. Are there, if any, deficiencies in both content and structure of the above treaty?
4. What is your idea to improve the above treaty?

联合国海洋法公约

序言

本公约缔约各国，

本着以互相谅解和合作的精神解决与海洋法有关的一切问题的愿望，并且认识到本公约对于维护和平、正义和全世界人民的进步做出重要贡献的历史意义，

注意到自从一九五八年和一九六〇年在日内瓦举行了联合国海洋法会议以来的种种发展，着重指出了需要有一项新的可获一般接受的海洋法公约，

意识到各海洋区域的种种问题都是彼此密切相关的，有必要作为一个整体来加以考虑，

认识到有需要通过本公约，在妥为顾及所有国家主权的情形下，为海洋建立一种法律秩序，以便利国际交通和促进海洋的和平用途，海洋资源的公平而有效的利用，海洋生物资源的养护以及研究、保护和保全海洋环境，

考虑到达成这些目标将有助于实现公正公平的国际经济秩序，这种秩序将照顾到全人类的利益和需要，特别是发展中国家的特殊利益和需要，不论其为沿海国或内陆国，

希望以本公约发展一九七〇年十二月十七日第2749（XXV）号决议所载各项原则，联合国大会在该决议中庄严宣布，除其他外，国家管辖范围以外的海床和洋底区域及其底土以及该区域的资源为人类的共同继承财产，其勘探与开发应为全人类的利益而进行，不论各国的地理位置如何，

相信在本公约中所达成的海洋法的编纂和逐渐发展，将有助于按照《联合国宪章》所载的联合国的宗旨和原则巩固各国间符合正义和权利平等原则的和平、安全、合作和友好关系，并将促进全世界人民的经济

和社会方面的进展，

确认本公约未予规定的事项，应继续以一般国际法的规则和原则为准据，

经协议如下：

……

第二部分　领海和毗连区

第一节　一般规定

第二条　领海及其上空、海床和底土的法律地位

1. 沿海国的主权及于其陆地领土及其内水以外邻接的一带海域，在群岛国的情形下则及于群岛水域以外邻接的一带海域，称为领海。

2. 此项主权及于领海的上空及其海床和底土。

3. 对于领海的主权的行使受本公约和其他国际法规则的限制。

第二节　领海的界限

第三条　领海的宽度

每一国家有权确定其领海的宽度，直至从按照本公约确定的基线量起不超过十二海里的界限为止。

第四条　领海的外部界限

领海的外部界限是一条其每一点同基线最近点的距离等于领海宽度的线。

第五条　正常基线

除本公约另有规定外，测算领海宽度的正常基线是沿海国官方承认的大比例尺海图所标明的沿岸低潮线。

第六条　礁石

在位于环礁上的岛屿或有岸礁环列的岛屿的情形下，测算领海宽度的基线是沿海国官方承认的海图上以适当标记显示的礁石的向海低潮线。

……

第三〇六条　批准和正式确认

本公约须经各国和第三〇五条第1款（b）、（c）、（d）和（e）项

所指的其他实体批准，并经该条第 1 款（f）项所指的实体按照附件九予以正式确认。批准书和正式确认书应交存于联合国秘书长。

第三〇七条 加入

本公约应持续开放给各国和第三〇五条所指的其他实体加入。第三〇五条第 1 款（f）项所指的实体应按照附件九加入。加入书应交存于联合国秘书长。

第三〇八条

1. 本公约应自第六十份批准书或加入书交存之日后十二个月生效。

2. 对于在第六十份批准书和加入书交存以后批准或加入本公约的每一国家，在第 1 款限制下，本公约应在该国将批准书或加入书交存后第三十天起生效。

3. 管理局大会应在本公约生效之日开会，并应选举管理局的理事会。如果第一六一条的规定不能严格适用，则第一届理事会应以符合该条目的的方式组成。

4. 筹备委员会草拟的规则、章程和程序，应在管理局按照第十一部分予以正式通过以前暂时适用。

5. 管理局及其各机关应按照关于预备性投资的第三次联合国海洋法会议决议二以及筹备委员会依据该决议做出的各项决定行事。

第三〇九条 保留和例外

除非本公约其他条款明示许可，对本公约不得做出保留或例外。

（文献来源：http: //www. un. org/zh/law/sea/los/index. shtml，检索日期：2016 年 7 月 15 日。）

Reading Comprehension

Directions: Please give brief answers to the following questions.

1. 该条约表达了什么主旨？
2. 在格式上，该条约由几部分组成？
3. 分析该条约对于各签约国和平利用海洋资源的意义。

6. 2 Regulation
第二节 条例

Basic Knowledge
一、基础知识

Introduction

A regulation is a legal norm used to prescribe or proscribe conduct, to calibrate incentives, or to change preferences.

In statist mechanisms it can also be extended to monitoring and enforcement of rules as established by primary or delegated legislation. In this form, it is generally a written instrument containing rules having the force of statist law (as opposed to natural law).

In general, regulations are written by executive agencies as a way to enforce laws passed by the legislature.

(一) 简介

条例是国家权力机关或行政机关依照政策和法令而制定并发布的，针对政治、经济、文化等各个领域内的某些具体事项而作出的，比较全面系统、具有长期执行效力的法规性公文。国际条例是一国在对外交往的过程中由国家权力机关制定的处理对外政治、经济、文化诸领域外交事务的规范性文件。

Contents and Features

Different countries may employ various ways and formats in writing regulations, but three parts are generally found in all regulations: title, body and signature. The title should have a theme and a record type. The signature is the date when the regulation is passed, announced and carried out. The body should include the cause, content and the requirements of the regulation.

（二）内容和特点

条例一般由标题、签署、正文三部分组成，有以下特点：

1. 内容的法规性

条例是国家机关为控制或调整国际关系中某些方面的准则而使用的立法性手段，是基本法律制定以前的单项法规，又是制定以后、贯彻实施之前的具体化与细则化，用以保证基本法律的具体实施。条例一经颁布实施，其所涉及的对象，必须依条款办事，否则将要受到法律、行政或经济的处理。

2. 时效的稳定性

条例一经颁布实施，在一个相当长时限内，对其所涉及的对象行为起约束作用。

3. 制发的独特性

除社会团体内部制定的针对内部成员的工作条例外，其他条例制发者必须是国家权力机关或行政机关以及受这些机关委派的组织。

（张浩，2014）

Writing Requirement

The writing of regulation should be brief and adhere to format requirements. The reason should be stated at the beginning. It goes like this: "The regulation is made in order to…" As for the body, the rules should be followed by examples. The requirements, the effective date and the power of interpretation and amendment should be elaborated at the end.

（三）写作要求

1. 条例的写作必须符合国家法规，符合党的方针政策。制定条例时，要以维护国家、集体的根本利益为前提，所以在制定前，要充分进行调查研究，充分领会国家的有关政策精神和本地区、本单位的实际情况，不能有疏漏。

2. 条例的种类很多，必须要有明确的权限。要注意条例的使用范围，不可越权制定。

3. 条例的最大特点是分条例项，条目要从头贯到底，所以要注意结构严谨、条目清晰。凡经有关部门或会议肯定的，首先要把内容和事项搞清楚，抓住主要问题和基本精神，采取分章、分条、分款的办法，用简洁、准确、具体的文字，把内容一一表达清楚、明白，切不可模棱两可、含糊不清，更不能有遗漏，特别要注意，未经决定或有分歧的意见，一概不可写入条例中。

4. 写作条例时应注意的问题：（1）要依据党规国法和自身的法定权限；（2）不仅要写明准许什么、不准许什么，还要写明违反的处理规定；（3）概念要明确，不允许有不同的解释。

（张浩，2014）

Case Studies

二、案例分析

案例一

中华人民共和国外交特权与豁免条例

（一九八六年九月五日第六届全国人民代表大会
常务委员会第十七次会议通过一九八六年九月五日
中华人民共和国主席令第四十四号公布施行）

第一条　为确定外国驻中国使馆和使馆人员的外交特权与豁免，便于外国驻中国使馆代表其国家有效地执行职务，特制定本条例。

第二条　使馆外交人员原则上应当是具有派遣国国籍的人。如果委派中国或者第三国国籍的人为使馆外交人员，必须征得中国主管机关的同意。中国主管机关可以随时撤销此项同意。

第三条 使馆及其馆长有权在使馆馆舍和使馆馆长交通工具上，使用派遣国的国旗或者国徽。

第四条 使馆馆舍不受侵犯。中国国家工作人员进入使馆馆舍，须经使馆馆长或者其授权人员同意。中国有关机关应当采取适当措施，保护使馆馆舍免受侵犯或者损害，使馆的馆舍、设备及馆舍内其他财产和使馆交通工具免受搜查、征用、扣押或者强制执行。

第五条 使馆馆舍免纳捐税，但为其提供特定服务的费用不在此限。使馆办理公务所收规费和手续费免纳捐税。

中华人民共和国外交部

（文献来源：黄金祺编：《英汉对照外交文献文书教程》（下册），世界知识出版社 2004 年版，第 152－156 页。）

分析概要

这份条例从结构上看，由标题、正文、签署三部分组成。其正文部分对内容进行逐条说明，是条例的主体部分，交代了因由、条规和例外情况，并且说明条例所涉及对象的有关范围。

案例二

Regulations of the People's Republic of China on the Installation and Use of Radio Stations by Foreign Diplomatic Missions in China

April 1982

1. The Government of the People's Republic of China handles the matter relating to the installation of radio transmitter receiver stations in Beijing by foreign diplomatic missions in China in accordance with the principle

of reciprocity. Foreign diplomatic missions desiring to install radio transmitter receiver stations in Beijing must apply by addressing a note to the Ministry of Foreign Affairs of the People's Republic of China for such installation and must fill in the attached Registration Form for Radio Stations Operated by Diplomatic Missions in China and send it in duplicate to the Ministry of Foreign affairs of the People's Republic of China. Radio stations may be installed and used only with permission.

2. Any changes in technical data itemized in the attached registration form, which may be during the course of operation of radio transmitter receiver stations already installed by foreign diplomatic missions with the permission of the Government of the People's Republic of China, should promptly be notified to the Ministry of Foreign Affairs of the People's Republic of China.
3. Foreign diplomatic missions in China wishing to import new radio transmitter receiver stations or replacements for worn-out equipment should likewise submit to the Ministry Foreign Affairs of the People's Republic of China in duplicate full technical data as required by the attached form. These may be imported only with permission.

（文献来源：黄金祺编：《英汉对照外交文献文书教程》（下册），世界知识出版社2004年版，第152－156页。）

Analysis

This regulation is addressed to foreign diplomatic missions who aim at installing radio stations in China, as is indicated in the title. In terms of structure, it consists of title, date and body. As the major part, the body makes clear Chinese government's stand and conditions on which radio stations are allowed to be installed in China.

Supplementary Readings
三、拓展阅读

请阅读以下条例并回答问题。

Regulations on Border Inspection

Article 1 With a view to safeguarding the sovereignty and national security of the People's Republic of China and facilitating the entry and exit of persons and means of transportation, Frontier Inspection Stations are set up at ports, airports, border railway stations and other border thoroughfares open to international traffic as well as other specially designated ports of entry and exit.

……

Article 4 All person entering or leaving the country shall present their passports or other certificates for entry and exit to the Frontier Inspection Stations for examination.

Frontier Inspection Stations shall deny entry or exit to those who refuse to present for examination their passports or other certificates for entry and exit. In the ease of those whose passports or other certificates for entry or exit are at variance with China's regulations governing entry and exit, Frontier Inspection Stations shall deny them entry or exit, or require them to go through the necessary procedures for entry or exit.

Article 5 All persons entering or leaving the country shall submit their luggage and other personal belongings to the Frontier Inspection Stations for inspection.

The luggage and other personal belongings of foreign diplomatic and consular officers and other persons enjoying immunities shall be dealt with by the Frontier Inspection Stations in accordance with the relevant regulations of the People's Republic of China.

Article 6 The captain of a ship entering or leaving the country shall submit lists of the crew and passengers to the Frontier Inspection Stations and subject his ship with all persons on board to their inspection.

Crew members and other persons, when embarking and disembarking the ship, shall present their valid permits to the Frontier Inspection Stations for examination and clearance.

……

Article 7 The captain of an aircraft entering or leaving the country shall submit lists of the crew and passengers to the Frontier Inspection Stations and subject the aircraft with all persons on board to their inspection.

An aircraft entering the country before landing at a designated airport or all aircraft leaving the country after taking off from a designated airport but before crossing the border may not land or airdrop persons or articles en route. In case of a forced landing or airdropping of persons or articles en route necessitated by emergency or accident, the captain of the aircraft shall immediately report the details and reasons to the Frontier Inspection Station or local public security authorities through a civil airport.

Article 8 The train conductor or train guard of a passenger or freight train entering or leaving the country shall declare to the Frontier Inspection Station the numbers of his crew and passengers and the formation of the train and shall submit the train with all persons on board to inspection by the Frontier Inspection Station.

Trains entering or leaving the country, while traveling between the national boundary and the border station of the People's Republic of China, may not take aboard or discharge any person or cargo or make uncalled for stops en route.

……

Article 11 Violators of these regulations shall be dealt with by the Frontier Inspection Stations according to law and on the merits of each specific case.

Article 12 These Regulations shall enter into force upon the day of their publication.

（文献来源：黄金祺编：《英汉对照外交文献文书教程》（下册），世界知识出版社 2004 年版，第 4－7 页。）

Reading Comprehension

Directions: In this part, you will have to go over the passage quickly and choose the best answer from the four choices marked A, B, C and D.

1. From the structure, which part was missing in this passage?
   A. Title
   B. specific regulations
   C. signature
   D. both A and C
2. Which of the following statement is not true?
   A. All persons and means of transportation shall enter or leave the county through the ports, airports, border railway stations and other border thoroughfares.
   B. Violators of these regulations shall be dealt with by the Frontier Inspection Stations according to law and on the merits of each specific case.
   C. All persons entering or leaving the country shall submit their luggage and other personal belongings to the Frontier Inspection Stations for inspection.
   D. Persons with privilege entering or leaving the country may not observe the laws and decrees.
3. What is the main theme of this passage?
   A. Border inspection
   B. Diplomatic privileges and immunities
   C. Trade clause

D. Boundary treaty

中华人民共和国对外合作开采海洋石油资源条例
（一九八二年一月三十日公布）

第一章　总则

第一条　为促进国民经济的发展，扩大国际经济技术合作，在维护国家主权和经济利益的前提下允许外国企业参与合作开采中华人民共和国海洋石油资源，特制定本条例。

第二条　中华人民共和国的内海、领海、大陆架以及其他属于中华人民共和国海洋资源管辖海域石油资源，都属于中华人民共和国国家所有。

在前款海域内，为开采石油而设置的建筑物、构筑物、作业船舶，以及相应的陆岸油（气）集输终端和基地，都受中华人民共和国管辖。

第三条　中国政府依法保护参与合作开采海洋石油资源的外国企业的投资、应得利润和其他合法权益，依法保护外国企业的合作开采活动。

在本条例范围内，合作开采海洋石油资源的一切活动，都应当遵守中华人民共和国的法律、法令和国家的有关规定；参与实施石油作业的企业和个人，都应当受中国法律的约束，接受中国政府有关主管部门的检查、监督。

……

第二十四条　作业者和承包者在实施石油作业中，应当遵守中华人民共和国有关环境保护和安全方面的法律规定，并参照国际惯例进行作业，保护渔业资源和其他自然资源，防止对大气、海洋、河流、湖泊和陆地等环境的污染和损害。

……

第三十条　本条例的施行细则由石油工业部制定。

第三十一条　本条例自公布之日起施行。

（文献来源：黄金祺编：《英汉对照外交文献文书教程》（下册），世界知识出版社 2004 年版，第 117－122 页。）

Reading Comprehension

Directions: Please give brief answers to the following questions.

1. 该条例的主旨是什么？颁布该条例要达到何种目的？
2. 请简述该条例的主要内容。
3. 从格式上看，该条例是否符合要求？有无需要补充的地方？
4. 分析该条例对维护国家主权与利益的意义。

6.3 Exercises
课后练习

- **True or False**

Directions: Read the following sentences and decide whether they are true or false.

1. In the broad sense, treaty may be taken to cover all international engagements concluded between states governed by international law in the form of written instruments.
2. Treaties can be concluded in the name of heads of state, between states or governments.
3. Treaties of "mutual guarantee" are not international compacts.
4. In general, regulations are written by executive agencies as a way to enforce laws passed by the legislature.
5. Regulations constitute an important category of diplomatic documents because they involve international relations.
6. Treaties in head of state form are more informal than in other forms.
7. Foreign-related laws and regulations are formulated in conformity with

international law and usage and in the light of the respective internal laws and policies of different states.

• Gap-filling

Directions: Complete each sentence with appropriate words.

1. A treaty between two nations is called ________; one among three nations or more is called ________.
2. A treaty usually comes with a term of ________, and it ________ if not extended.
3. Bilateral treaties should be prepared in ________ for signing, so that each party can save a ________ of the original one after the signing of the treaty.

• Multiple Choices

Directions: In this part there are several incomplete sentences. For eachsentence there are four choices marked A, B, C and D. Choose the ONE answer that best completes the sentence.

1. A treaty is an agreement under international law entered into by actors in international law, namely ________.
   A. sovereign states and international organizations
   B. countries
   C. states
   D. city
2. A multilateral treaty is concluded among ________.
   A. several countries　　B. two states
   C. several cities　　D. two countries
3. In which ways can treaties be loosely compared to contracts?
   A. both are not applicable until the past century.
   B. both are means of willing parties assuming obligations among them-

selves.

C. a party to either that fails to live up to their obligations can be held liable under international law.

D. both B and C

4. In general, regulations are written by ________ as a way to enforce laws passed by the legislature.

A. executive agencies B. legal organization

C. government D. official workers

5. Any independent and sovereign state has its own laws and regulations governing ________.

A. foreign diplomatic missions

B. consular posts and their personnel

C. other foreign nationals staying or residing in its territory

D. all of above

• Translation

Directions: translate the following sentences into the target language.

English-Chinese Translation

1. The Contracting Parties have agreed that wherever the boundary follows a river, the midstream line shall be the boundary.
2. The Contracting Parties have agreed that any dispute concerning the boundary which may arise after the formal delimitation of the boundary between the two countries shall be settled by the two Parties through friendly consultations.
3. The present Treaty shall remain in force for ten years and thereafter shall continue to be in force until terminated in accordance with the provisions of Paragraph 2 of this Article.
4. The member of the mission shall enjoy freedom of movement and travel within Chinese territory except for areas the entry into which is

prohibited or restricted by the regulations of the Chinese Government.

5. The diplomatic missions and their members may bring and import firearms and bullets into China for their personal use, subject to the approval of the Chinese government and to its relevant regulations.

Chinese-English translation

1. 任何一个独立自主的国家都有它自己的涉及外国使、领馆及其人员以及在本国居住和停留的外国人的法律和规定。

2. 中国作为一个独立自主和发展中的社会主义国家，在共和国成立以来也制定过一系列涉外法规。

3. 进出国境的人员，必须遵守中华人民共和国的法令和边防检查制度。

4. 对于违反本条例的人员，边防检查站应当根据情节，依法予以处理。

5. 为维护中华人民共和国的主权、安全和社会秩序，有利于发展国际交往，特制定本法。

• Simulative Exercise

Suppose China is going to sign a boundary treaty with Pakistan, please write a boundary treaty to define the specific boundary limits between the People's Republic of China and Pakistan.

7　Documents for Commercial Affairs

第七章　商务文书

Abstract

With the expansion of globalization, the trade between countries is prospering. As a result, the business documents are more and more popular. Therefore, it is necessary to introduce the documents for commercial affairs.

Documents for commercial affairs are the official documents in business affairs. They are produced in the business activities. As they carry important information and records, they have strict and standard format. Therefore, they are indispensable in modern enterprise management.

There are many kinds of business documents. But in this chapter we will only focus on the business letter of intent, the order confirmation, the contract and the authorization. These will help us understand the format and principles of business document writing, so as to better convey and implement the enterprise requirements and enhance the international competitiveness of multinational companies.

内容概览

全球化的扩展使得各国之间的贸易不断增多，商务文书在国际上的使用也越来越频繁，成为对外交往中的一种文书类型。

商务文书是商业事务中的公务文书，是企业在生产经营管理活动中产生的，是按照严格的、既定的生效程序和规范的格式制定的具有传递信息和记录作用的载体。它是企业经营运作的信息载体，是贯彻企业执行力的重要保障性因素。规范严谨的商务文书已经成为现代跨国企业管理的基础。

本章重点介绍商务意向书、成交确认书、合同和授权书这几类商务文书，以期帮助读者深入了解商务公文写作的原则、格式和技巧，规范日常工作中的商务公文写作，以便更好地落实和传达企业要求，提高跨国企业持续的国际竞争力。

7.1 Business Letter of Intent
第一节 商务意向书

Basic Knowledge
一、基础知识

Introduction

In business, a letter of intent is a letter from one company to another acknowledging a willingness and ability to do business. A letter of intent is not a contract and cannot be enforced; it is just a document stating serious intent to carry out certain business activities. It means all the agreement and conditions that have been discussed between two parties or people before an agreement are finalized. It contains all the important aspects of the agreement and the conduct of the two parties on a contract. A letter of intent is signed for legality and for the intention of declaring that two parties involved are negotiating an agreement.

The most common purposes of a letter of intent are:

1. To clarify the key points of a complex transaction for the convenience of the parties;
2. To declare officially that the parties are currently negotiating, as in a

merger or joint-venture proposal;

3. To provide safeguards in case a deal collapses during negotiation;
4. To verify certain issues regarding payments done for someone else, e. g. credit card payments.

（一）简介

商务意向书是在交易商尚未最后达成协议前，买卖双方针对某一合作项目，为达成某项交易，将共同争取实现目标的设想和意愿，有时还包括初步商定的部分交易条件，记录于一份书面文件上。这种书面文件可称之为商务意向书，简称“意向书”。商务意向书是对某个合作项目或某笔交易共同感兴趣的各方经过初步接触和洽谈后，为表示进一步合作、正式谈判的意愿所签订的文件。它往往显示了各方的诚意和意愿，同时也对各方的合作起着积极的促进作用。它主要用于洽谈重要的合作项目和涉外经营项目，如合资经营企业、合作经营贸易、承包国际工程等方面，可以在企业与企业之间、地区和地区之间、国家和国家之间等使用。

商务意向书的作用如下：

首先，具有邀约作用，有助于合作各方进一步做实质性的接触和谈判。这种邀约性可使任何一方主动邀请对方进行了解和考察，以便进行更密切和深入的谈判。

其次，商务意向书是项目合作、交易达成的最初蓝本。无论是从内容还是形式上，意向书与合同等其他商务文书都有关联，有利于促使正式“协议书”或“合同”的签订。

再次，商务意向书具有道义上的约束力。它是经济合作由初期的商洽转向实质性谈判的基础依据，有利于促进谈判的深入。

（戴萍，2007）

Contents and Features

Letters of intent resemble written contracts, but are usually not binding on the parties in their entirety. Many letters of intent, however, contain provisions that are binding, such as non-disclosure agreements or a covenant to negotiate in good faith or a “stand-still” provision promising exclusive rights to negotiate. A letter of intent may sometimes be interpreted by a court of law as binding the parties to it, if it too-closely resembles a formal contract. So if carefully negotiated, a letter of intent may serve to protect both parties to a transaction. For example, a seller of a business may insert what’s known as a “no solicitation” provision which would prevent the buyer from subsequently hiring an employee of the seller’s business should the two parties not be able to close the transaction. On the other hand, a letter of intent may protect the buyer of a business by imposing a condition to complete the transaction on their part if financing the deal is not obtained.

（二）内容和特点

从内容来看，商务意向书有以下特点：

1. 简略性与临时性

正式合同和协议书等要求行文用词严谨，条款约定详细，一般将潜在的问题都考虑进去。而意向书只是传达“意向”，提请对方注意或供参考，因此在内容及表达上一般较合同更为简洁。意向书只是表达谈判的初步成果，为今后谈判做铺垫；一旦谈判深入，最终确定了合作双方的权利和义务，其使命也就结束了。

2. 原则性与意向性

只有各方对某个合作项目或某笔交易具有共同的兴趣，而且通过初步接触和洽谈后，各方都有进一步合作谈判的诚意，才会签订书面意向。它反映了合作当事人对合作事宜的共同、初步的意向，不是合作时具体的实施方案。但当事人要进一步商洽实质性合作事宜，应该以意向书为基础，因此意向书是深入合作的原则性文件，可以为以后签订正式的合同或协议书做好必要的准备，能推进合作的顺利进行。

3. 协商性与灵活性

意向书是经过当事人初步的协商后才产生的，如果一方当事人觉得其中有不妥当之处，仍可通过再次协商与合作达成共识。意向书正因为具有这种协商性，所以十分灵活，在内容上十分笼统、粗略，为下一步实质性谈判留出了足够的斡旋余地。

4. 一致性

意向书虽然只是谈判某一阶段而不是最后阶段的成果，但其内容应是经过协商双方一致同意的，能表达双方的共同意愿。由于具备了一致性，意向书才成为双方认可的今后谈判的基础。

5. 非法律性与信誉性

商务意向书仅仅是表明各方共同希望或拟将进行的某一行为，尤其是在涉外经济贸易中，意向书的内容没有明确的要约和承诺，只能视为要约的邀请。因此，尽管双方在该文件上签了字，也不受法律的约束。不过，虽然意向书无法律强制执行力，但仍有一定的约束力，对于当事人信誉的维护和提升有很大的影响，直接关系到是否有下一次合作或另外的合作方。值得注意的是，一些大陆法系国家认为意向书对当事人也具有约束力。在与这类国家签意向书时，对于此，中文应有明确说明，以避免误解和被动。

（吴瑞玲，2013；戴萍，2007）

Writing Requirements

Remember that when writing a letter of intent, the words, letters and style should be appropriate to the situation intended for the letter you are about to write. All of the things you would write must be factual and straight to the point but with modesty and respect to the people you are writing to. And also be sure that you must carry out all of the things you will write, which may be an oath, promise or condition you swear to the people you are writing to.

（三）写作要求

首先，商务意向书的写作要充分表达双方的意愿，态度一定要诚恳，语气一定要友好、委婉，不得使用“必须”“否则”“一定”等有强制性、要挟意味的词语。其次，要以认真负责的态度来对待，它虽然不是一个具有法律效力的文件，但它是双方愿意合作的第一个文件，也是进行谈判、实施合作的依据，因此应该怀着认真负责的态度来撰写。

商务意向书一般由标题、正文和落款三部分组成。格式可以参照合同的写法。

1. 标题

商务意向书的标题由合作内容、合作方式或项目名称、文种组成。有三种写法：第一种完全式，由合作单位名称、合作项目名称和文种组成，如《××股份有限公司与××集团技术转让意向书》。第二种半完全式，常由合作项目名称和文种构成，如《产品研发意向书》。第三种是简便式，即直接以“意向书”为题。

2. 正文

正文包括前言、主体、结尾三部分。

（1）前言。前言即正文的开头部分。一般写明合作双方在何时、何地就什么项目进行洽谈，包括合作的依据、原因或目的。双方单位要写全称，同时为了行文简洁，往往将中方单位居前，并用括号注明“简称甲方”；将外方单位居后，并用括号注明“简称乙方”。洽谈代表要写明身份、职务、姓名。如果是涉外意向书，则还要写明注册国家、法定地址、营业执照编号和副本、法人代表的姓名、国籍和职务等。这部分最后用“现将有关意向归纳如下”或“……达成意向如下”作为承上启下的惯用语句结束来引出正文的主体。

（2）主体。主体是商务意向书的中心内容，主要将双方商谈、认可的事项和达成的意见以分条归纳的方式表述出来。意向书只是一种意愿的表达，因此主体的条文没有严格的程序要求，一般是将共同关注的条文放在前面。一般来说，其内容主要包括：

合作项目的范围、交易对象。合作项目的范围、交易对象包括生产经营的主要产品的类别，以及交易货物的主要品种、规格等。

投资数额或成交价格。投资数额包括投资总额和双方出资数额。投资额的货币单位要求统一。可用双方任何一方国家的货币单位，也可用双方认可的第三国货币单位。双边计算了投资总额后，还应写明双方出资的数额和各方所占投资总额的比例。成交价格包括单价和总金额。

合作或交易双方的名称与地址。名称与地址均写全称。选定合作地址的，应写明包括有国名的详细地址；尚未选定的，应注明大致区域。

产品销售方式或交易方式。产品销售方式包括内销和外销的比例以及各方各自负责的销售比例。

（3）结尾。要写明进一步的洽谈打算，即今后工作的进度，这是意向书不可缺少的内容，代表了各方进一步谈判的意愿。通常在最后注明一句："未尽事宜，在双方正式签订合同或协议时另行补充。"

3. 落款

包括甲、乙双方单位的名称，双方代表的职务、姓名及签署年月日。有时，有的意向书还要注明联系人姓名、联系电话、联系地址等，一些要报上级部门批准立项的意向书还要写明报送单位。

（戴萍，2007；吴瑞玲，2013）

Case Studies
二、案例分析

（一）买方购货意向书

Letter of Intent

June 20, 2013

Kate Anderson

Kate's Cupcakes, Inc.

Dear Ms. Anderson,

We welcome the opportunity to submit a proposal to acquire the business of Kate's Cupcakes, Inc. and related companies (collectively the "Company" or "Seller") operatingapproximately 15 retail stores in California selling baked goods (the "Business"). We understand the desire to proceed expeditiously with a sale of the Business. We are prepared to move quickly on the transaction and believe we are well suited to do so. This letter summarizes our proposal.

1. Purchase Price

An entity newly formed by Pearson, LLC ("Buyer") would purchase substantially all of the operating assets, including all tangible and intangible assets, equipment, leases, contract rights, and intellectual property used in the Business for a purchase price of one million one hundred thousand dollars ($1,100,000). Buyer will not assume any liabilities of the Business of the Company other than liabilities accruing after the closing under contracts or leases assumed by Buyer.

2. Definitive Agreement

The closing will be subject to the negotiation and execution of definitive transaction documents that will include, among other things, customary representations, warranties, covenants, and indemnities by the Seller and their principals regarding the business, operations, and financial condition of the Business.

3. Closing Date

The parties acknowledge that time is of importance and that they will work towards closing the transaction as quickly as possible.

4. Conditions to Closing

The consummation of the Transaction will be subject to the satisfaction of customary conditions, including, without limitation, the following:

a. The negotiation, execution, and delivery of definitive agreements satisfactory to each of the parties, including retail leases, and securing of any required governmental or third party approvals, waivers, or consents.

b. Maintenance of the Company's business in the ordinary course, and the absence of any material adverse change in the Company's business of financial condition or material changed in the conduct of its business as of the date of this Letter of Intent.

c. The Company not seeking or requesting any type of bankruptcy protection or bankruptcy procedure.

5. Binding Agreement

Other than this paragraph 5, which is intended to be and is legally binding, this letter is nonbinding and constitutes an indication of intent only and creates no liability or obligation of any nature whatsoever among the parties hereto with respect to any contemplated transaction or anyother matter or action described or referred to herein. Legally binding obligations with respect to the contemplated transaction will only arise upon execution of a definitive agreement and related agreements with respect to the transaction.

If the foregoing is satisfactory, please indicate your agreement with the foregoing by countersigning a copy of this letter and returning it to our attention. We look forward to proceeding together on this transaction.

Michael D. Kampfer
Managing Director
mkampfer@pearsonllc. com
662. 555. 0198

By:

Its:

（文献来源：http: //www. tidyforms. com/download/letter-of-intent-for-business/redirect/pdf. html, 检索日期：2016 年 1 月 23 日。）

Analysis

The business letter of intent, with its title, body and signature, includes necessary information for both sides. It states clearly the purpose and relevant information of appeals of both parties in proper details.

（二）合作意向书

甲方：×××公司

乙方：上海服务网

甲、乙双方通过协商达成以下合作意向：

1. 为了更好地服务于上海市民，让人们能在“上海服务网”上尽快找到需要的服务，甲方委托乙方在“上海服务网”上刊登介绍自己服务特色的文稿。刊登内容详见“刊登内容表”。

2. 乙方同意按甲方“刊登内容表”的内容在“上海服务网”上给予刊登介绍，如发现“刊登内容表”上有明显错误的地方，乙方可以予以更正。甲方对刊登出来的内容有异议，应及时通知乙方予以更正。

3. 甲方要对“刊登内容表”的真实性和提供的图片、照片负完全责任，也要对以后为客户提供的服务或产品质量负完全责任。乙方没有对甲方情况审核的权利和义务，所以不承担任何连带的责任。

4. 乙方不以盈利为目的，免费为甲方编录、刊登简介文稿。但考虑到网站运行需要费用，所以象征性地收取甲方每月 10 元的网络空间占用费，初期不满一个月的免费刊登，从下一个自然月开始收费。

5. 甲方可以随时终止支付网络空间占用费，乙方一般不会把刊登上去的简介文稿撤下来，除非网站空间不够或甲方书面要求撤除，目的是为上海市民多提供一些服务信息。搜索排行顺序按刊登先后以及星值大小连续安排。

6. 刊登内容表（如有图片或照片、多个服务网点地址以及需要详细介绍，请另外传送，它们作为附加合作内容部分）。

刊登名称：	行业类型：
网站或 E－mail 地址：	业务联系人：
特色简介：	
联系电话：	是否提供电话联系上门服务的功能：
服务网点地址：	邮政编码：

7. 其他合作意向：如有其他合作意向，将另外签署“附加合作意向书”。

本“合作意向书”经双方签名盖章后的传真、复印件都有效。

甲方：×××公司	乙方：上海服务网
负责人签字：	负责人签字：
签署日期：	签署日期：

（文献来源：金波主编：《职业经理商务写作能力训练》，高等教育出版社 2004 年版，第 230－232 页。）

分析概要

这是一份某公司与上海服务网达成的商务意向书，该意向书以条款的方式呈现，其中还穿插了表格，使人一目了然，明确表达了双方的意愿和合作的范围与内容。为了保护商业隐私，没有把一些具体细节展示出来，但必要的条款是齐全的，值得借鉴。

Supplementary Readings

三、拓展阅读

阅读以下意向书，回答问题。

Letter of Intent for Possible Sale of Assets

Possible Seller:

Possible Buyer:

Business:

Date:

This is a non-binding letter of intent that contains provisions that are being discussed for a possible sale of the business named above from the possible Seller named above to the possible Buyer named above. This is not a contract. This is not a legally binding agreement. This is merely an outline of possible contract terms for discussion purpose only. This is being signed in order to enable the Possible Buyer to apply for financing of the purchase price. This letter of intent is confidential and shall not be disclosed to anyone other than the parties and their employees, attorneys and accountants and the possible lenders of the Possible Buyer. The terms of the transaction being discussed are attached hereto, but the terms (and the possible sale itself) are not binding unless and until they are set forth in a written contract signed by Possible Seller and Possible Buyer. The word "shall" is used in the attached terms only as an example of how a contract might read, and it does not mean that the attached terms are or ever will be legally binding.

____

____

Witness

（文献来源：陈永国、郑淑媛、陈智钢：《新编英语应用文写作》，江西高校出版社2009年版，第93页。）

Reading Comprehension

Directions: Please give brief answers to the following questions.

1. What's the difference between this letter of intent and the samples in the part of case studies?
2. Based on the information provided, can you fill up the blanks for this letter of intent?

地产项目合作意向书

甲方：________________（以下简称甲方）
乙方：________________（以下简称乙方）
为使________________项目（以下简称本项目）在济南高新技术产业开发区实现产业化，根据国家及地方有关法律、法规，双方本着平等、自愿、有偿的原则，订立本协议。

一、土地问题

1. 土地位置及出让方式

甲方同意本项目进入济南出口加工区实现产业化。初步确定项目建设地点位于××，占地约×亩。其中独自使用面积×亩，代征道路面积×亩，确切位置坐标四至和土地面积待甲方规划土地建设管理部门实测后确认。甲方将国有土地使用权以有偿出让方式提供给乙方。

2. 土地价格

为体现对本项目的支持，甲方初步确定以×万元人民币/亩的优惠价格，将项目所需该宗土地的使用权出让给乙方，出让金总额为×万元人民币。该宗土地征用成本与出让值差额计×万元，由高新区参照项目单位纳税中高新区财政收益部分给予相同额度的扶持。

3. 付款方式

高新技术产业开发区规划土地建设管理部门与乙方签订正式土地使用权出让合同。乙方在该合同签订后十五日内，一次性向甲方付清土地使用权出让金。甲方收到全部土地使用权出让金后，按国家有关规定，尽快办妥国有土地使用证等有关手续。

二、其他

1. 在履行本协议时，若发生争议，双方协商解决；协商不成的，双方同意向济南市仲裁委员会申请仲裁，没有达成书面仲裁协议的，可向人民法院起诉。

2. 任何一方对于因发生不可抗力且自身无过错造成延误不能履行本协议有关条款之规定义务时，该种不履行将不构成违约，但当事一方必须采取一切必要的补救措施以减少造成的损失。并在发生不可抗力三十日内向另一方提交协议不能履行的或部分不能履行的，以及需延期的理由报告，同时，提供有关部门出具的不可抗力证明。

3. 本协议一式两份，甲、乙双方各执一份。两份协议具有同等法律效力，经甲、乙双方法定代表人（或委托代理人）签字盖章后生效。

4. 本协议于××年×月×日在中华人民共和国山东省济南市签订。

5. 本协议有效期限自××年×月×日起至××年×月×日止。

6. 本协议未尽事宜，双方可另行约定后作为本协议附件，与本协议具有同等法律效力。

甲方：（章）__________ 乙方：（章）__________

法定代表人（委托代理人）：__________

法定代表人（委托代理人）：__________

法人住所地：__________ 法人住所地：__________

邮政编码：__________ 邮政编码：__________

电话号码：__________ 电话号码：__________

（文献来源：http: //baike. baidu. com/link? url = Dbz-kN8XxgtfAyDbRk-GM9V2bd-e7DAQSdZ_S-ISjpT9RgG5iLrpfgp_LPO67exSZojNjH2k5pr ShiBkdY-GX-DnK, 检索日期：2016 年 1 月 30 日。）

Reading Comprehension

Directions: Please give brief answers to the following questions.

1. 该意向书合作的对象有哪些？

2. 该意向书由几部分构成?
3. 该意向书格式方面有何特点?

7.2 Order Confirmation
第二节 成交确认书

Basic knowledge
一、基础知识

Introduction

An order confirmation is a commercial document and the first official offer issued by a buyer to a seller, indicating types, quantities, and agreed prices for products or services. Acceptance of order confirmation by a seller forms a contract between the buyer and seller, so no contract exists until the order confirmation is accepted. It is used to control the purchasing of products and services from external suppliers.

Companies use order confirmations for several reasons:

1. Order confirmations allow buyers to clearly and explicitly communicate their intentions to sellers;
2. Sellers are protected in case of a buyer's refusal to pay for goods or services;
3. Order confirmations help a purchasing agent to manage incoming orders and pending orders;
4. Order confirmations provide economies in that they streamline the purchasing process to a standard procedure.

(一) 简介

成交确认书是买卖双方通过函电或口头谈判的交易，在成交后，卖方可以寄给对方列明达成交易的条件，作为书面证明的文件。成交确认书由卖方填制，一式两份，签字后交买方加签，然后各执一份，据以执行，它是我国对外贸易出口业务中所使用的一种合同形式，又称“销货确认书”“购货确认书”等。

成交确认书一般只言及交易商品的品名、品质、数量、价格、装运期及协议书中未规定的事项，这种成交确认书必须辅以协议书，才构成一个完整的契约。

成交确认书的作用在于它是办理进出口签证手续的重要文书，在各国法律上成交确认书有特别的效力，如果发生涉外贸易纠纷，可以以此为依据，取得经济保障。

（陈纪宁，2002）

Contents and Features

The typical contents of an order confirmation include the details of the ordered product or service like number of units and corresponding price, both contact and shipping addresses, the payment conditions and (if requested) the delivery date.

（二）内容和特点

成交确认书最主体的内容是交易双方关于此次交易产品和运输方式的具体信息，主要包括商品名称、规格、包装、数量、单价、金额、包装、交货期、装运港和目的港、付款方式、运输标志、商品检验等条款。除了交易双方交易产品的基本信息之外，在成交确认书中，盈利性的借款人或是金融机构为达成成交所提供一些金融服务也可以提及。比如，金融机构提供的像航运前后的保险、金融服务、国外订单支付、退款服务、订单确认等都可以在成交确认书中明确下来，为后期工作做铺垫。

成交确认书的各项条款是一个有机的整体，各个条款之间应前后呼应，相互衔接，保持一致，不应出现相互矛盾的内容。如商品品名，不能使用不同名称。单价、总值的货币必须相同。应详细列明卖方投保、投保金额、险别等内容。成交确认书各条款还要明确、完整和肯定，防止错列和漏列主要事项。文字要简练、严谨、明确，切忌使用模棱两可或含混不清的词句和文字，防止发生涉外贸易纠纷。

（向常华、叶昌德，2005）

Writing Requirement

The language of order confirmation should be accurate, complete and clear. Each clause should not be ambiguous and we should avoid the omission of main items. Order confirmation consists of three parts: beginning, body and ending.

1. Beginning. It includes the date of contract, the name of buyer and seller, and their addresses.
2. Body. This is the main part of the order confirmation, including the name of commodity, specifications, packing, quantity, unit price, total amount, delivery, port of loading and destination, payment terms, shipping marks, commodity inspection, insurance, and so on. Some of order confirmation also needs the special terms, such as arbitration or irresistible force.
3. Ending. It is the signature of the representatives of both parties.

（三）写作要求

成交确认书一般制作成信函的格式，只包括交易的主要条件，但不管它以信函方式或标准合同方式出现，只要当事人双方经磋商同意后签字，即成为正式的文件，具有法律约束力，双方必须按照其中内容行事，并成为日后抱怨、索赔的重要依据。其语言应力求严谨、准确，不得前后矛盾，并保持与洽谈协商内容的一致性。各条款是一个有机的整体，各个条款要明确、完整和肯定，防止错列和漏列主要事项，条款之间应前后呼应、相互衔接、保持一致。

成交确认书的写作内容由首部、正文、尾部等组成。

1. 首部

包括成交确认书的名称、号数、订约日期、订约地址、买卖双方的名称和地址，以及订约前的商洽函、电依据。中外客商在填写这部分内容时，要注意订约地点关系到外贸贸易纠纷是否适用于订约国的法律，不能随便填写，出口订约一般定为我国进出口公司所在地或定为中国。

2. 正文

这是成交确认书的主体部分，它较合同简单，内容一般包括商品名称、规格、包装、数量、单价、金额、交货期、装运港和目的港、付款方式、运输标志、商品检验、保险、备注等条款，有的还需要写明特约条款和一般条款，一般不列入异议索赔、仲裁、不可抗拒等条款。

3. 尾部

写明成交确认书的份数及保存，双方代表签字等。

（李笑，2009）

Case Studies
二、案例分析

案例一

Order Confirmation

NO. 239

Date: Nov. 6, 2001

Signed at: Tianjin

Sellers:

Address:

Tel:

Fax:

Dear Sir,

We hereby confirm having sold to you the following goods on terms and conditions as set forth below.

Commodity	Description	Quantity	Unit Price	Total Amount
110kV Double Circuit Pole in Straight Line	SGC − 33	3	85,732. 5	257197. 5
110Kv 90° Double Circuit Turning Pole	J90SG − 27	1	16,000	16,000

Packing

Time of Shipment: Within 30 days after your sight L/C arrived, allowing transshipment and partial shipment.

Terms of Payment: By confirmed and irrevocable L/C. for full invoice value, available by draft at sight, negotiable in Tianjin, valid in China until the 15th (fifteenth) day after date of shipment the L/C to reach sellers not later than Nov. 15, 2001

Insurance: To be effected by the buyer

Arbitration: All disputes in connection with this Contract or the execution thereof shall be settled amicably by negotiation. In case no settlement can be reached, the case under dispute may then be submitted to the China International Economic and Trade Arbitration Commission in Beijing for arbitration in accordance with the present valid rules of CIETAC when the case is applied. The arbitration fee shall be borne by the losing party unless otherwise awarded by the arbitration organization.

Remarks:

1. Shipping weight and quality should be certified by and subject to the inspection certificate issued by Tianjin Commodity Inspection Bureau.
2. All the terms contained in this S/C are to be deemed as final and the terms as well as wording to be specified in L/C shall be strictly in conformity with those as designated in this sales confirmation.

3. The buyer is requested to sign and return one copy of this Sales Confirmation immediately after receipt of the same.

Confirmed by the Buyer　　　　　　　　　　Confirmed by the seller

（文献来源：郑仰成主编：《电力英语应用文写作》，中国水利水电出版社 2003 年版，第 140－141 页。）

Analysis

This is a formal order confirmation, which states in details various information and related liability for both sides, laying foundation for the next step. It consists of three parts: the background of both sides, each expectation towards commodities and transportation, and the signature of both sides.

案例二

成交确认书

字第 369 号

日期：2000 年 7 月 18 日

签约地点：长沙

卖方：中国土产畜产进出口公司湖南省分公司

地址：中国湖南省长沙五一东路 13 号

电报挂号：长沙 “TUHSU”

买方：索卖有限公司

地址：英国伦敦西北区（2）索麦敦路 28 号

电报挂号：英国伦敦西北区（2）“CAMPE X WADR”, London NW2

买卖双方同意根据下列所定条件进行交易：

商品名称：白果

规格：一级

数量：10000 公斤

数量及总值均可有2%的增减，由卖方酌定。

单价：每公斤人民币8.80元

总值：人民币88000元

包装：用木箱装，外封草席，每箱净重20公斤

装运期：2001年11月1日前

装运口岸和目的地：由××市运至香港地区

保险：由买方缴付

付款条件：买方须于2001年10月25日前将保兑的、不可撤销的、可转让的和可分割的即期信用证开到卖方。信用证议付有效期延至上述装运期后15天，在广州到期。

装运标记：由卖方决定。

品质、数量、重量均以中国商品检验局或卖方所出的证明书为最后依据。

卖方	买方
（签字）	（签字）

（文献来源：祝雪虎：《经济文书写作技巧、模板与范例》，广东经济出版社2008年版，第368－369页。）

分析概要

这是中国土产畜产进出口公司湖南省分公司出售白果给索卖有限公司所达成的成交确认书。第一部分，详细介绍了签约的时间、地点、地址等信息。第二部分，明确了交易的产品、数量、价格、包装、运输等。第三部分是双方签字确认。整个结构完整清晰，值得参考。

Supplementary Readings
三、拓展阅读

阅读以下材料，思考问题。

Uline Order Confirmation 12/6/11 5:22 AM

ULINE 1-800-958-5463
SHIPPING SUPPLY SPECIALISTS

Order Summary

email print

Thank you for shopping with Uline. The following order was successfully submitted to Uline.
You will receive an e-mail confirmation after this order has been processed.

Order Number: **44811987**
Customer: 7209861
Purchase Order:

Order Date: 12/6/2011
Will Ship: 12/6/2011
Ship Via: FEDEX FRT

Billing Information
STRATFOR
221 W 6TH ST STE 400
AUSTIN, TX 78701-3426

Shipping Information
STRATFOR
221 W 6TH ST STE 400
AUSTIN, TX 78701-3426

Model #	Description	Unit Cost	Qty	Ext. Cost
S-14404TEX-M	NFL HOODIE-TEXANS M	Free / EA	1	FREE
S-343	12.5X12.5 WHT EZ FOLD 100/1600	$0.64 / EA	1000	$640.00
		SUBTOTAL=		$640.00
		TAX=		$57.83
		SHIPPING & HANDLING=		$60.95
		TOTAL=		**$758.78**

Special Instructions: LOADING DOCK IS BENEATH THE CHASE TOWER ON THE LAV ACA ST SIDE. THE CLEARANCE IS LOW (I THINK AROUND 13 FT)IF THE TRUCK IS TOO TALL THE PALLET WILL NEE D TO BE BROUGHT DOWN THE RAMP WITH A PALLET JACK. CALL AND WE WILL MEET THE DRIVER 512-744-4305.

（文献来源：https: //wikileaks. org/gifiles/attach/7/7861 _ Uline% 20Ord- er% 20Confirmation. pdf, 检索日期：2016 年 2 月 2 日。）

Reading Comprehension

Directions: Please give brief answers to the following questions.

1. How many parts does this order confirmation consist of?
2. What purpose of the order confirmation?
3. Can you generalize some language features of order confirmation?

成交确认书

×字第×号

日期：×年×月×日

签约地点：×市

卖方：中国山东省制药有限公司

地址：中国山东省济南市路号

买方：马来西亚有限公司

地址：马来西亚吉隆坡路号

买卖双方同意根据以下所定条件进行交易：

商品名称：科恒滴眼液

规格：5毫升装

数量：5000000盒

单价：每盒人民币3.8元

总值：人民币19000000元

包装：每100盒为一箱

装运期：2001年5月14日前

装运口岸和目的地：由济南市运至吉隆坡

保险：由买方缴付

付款条件：买方须于2001年5月1日前将保兑的、不可撤销的、可转让的和可分割的即期信用证开到卖方。信用证议付有效期延至上述装运期后15天，在济南到期。

装运标记由卖方决定。

品质、数量、重量均以中国商品检验局或卖方所出的证明书为最后依据。

（文献来源：黎孟德：《实用应用文大全：规范、实用、权威的应用文范文》，成都时代出版社2004年版，第431页。）

Reading Comprehension

Directions: Please give brief answers to the following questions.

1. 简述该篇成交确认书的主要内容。
2. 该篇成交确认书完整吗？我们可以怎么改进它？
3. 该篇成交确认书有何值得借鉴的地方？

7.3 Contract
第三节 合同

Basic Knowledge
一、基础知识

Introduction

A contract, in the simplest definition, is a promise enforceable by law. The promise may be to do something or to refrain from doing something. The making of a contract requires the mutual assent of two or more persons, one of them ordinarily making an offer and other accepting. If one of parties fails to keep the promises, the other is entitled to legal recourse against him. The law of contracts has to do with such questions as whether a contract exists, what the meaning of it is, whether a contract has been broken, and what compensation is due the injured party.

（*The New Encyclopaedia Briannica, Inc. 1977*）

（一）简介

合同是指两个或两个以上当事人为共同达到一定目的，按照法律规定，就确认各自的权利和义务关系而达成的一种协议。根据《中华人民共和国合同法》的规定，合同是指平等民事主体的法人、其他经济组织、个体工商户、农村承包经营户相互之间，为实现一定经济目的，明确相互权利义务关系而订立的合同。合同是平等主体之间设立的确定民事权利和义务的协议。它是一种承诺，违反该承诺可以得到法律救济，在某种意义上法律将履行该承诺也看成是一种责任。合同就是有法律约束力的协议。总而言之，合同是用以规定当事人的权利与义务，预防与解决争议的依据。

Contents and Features

The contract should be made by both two parties. According to the contract law set forth by China in 1999. The contract should include:

1. Titles or names of the parties and the domiciles thereof;
2. Date and place of signature of the contract;
3. Type of the contract and the kind, scope of the subject matter of the contract;
4. Technical conditions, quality, standard, specifications and quantities of the subject matter of the contract;
5. Time limit, place and method of performance;
6. Terms of price, amount and way of payment and various additional charges;
7. Whether the contract could be assigned or conditions for assignment;
8. Compensation and other liabilities for breach of the contract;
9. Ways of settlement of disputes in case of disputes arising from the contract;
10. Languages to be used in the contract and their effectiveness.

（董晓波，2012）

（二）内容和特点

商务合同，根据其繁简程度的不同，可以采用正式合同（Contract）、协议书（Agreement）、确认书（Confirmation）、备忘录（Memorandum）或订单（Order）等书面形式。

商务合同的主要特点包括：

1. 合同必须经过缔结各方的商洽和谈判，采用书面形式写成，并要经过当事者的签字或确认。

2. 以外事合同所涉及的内容多少和重要性而论，一般可以分为简单合同和复杂合同。

3. 合同的条文规定要全面、完整、切合实际，语言准确，语气肯定，责任规定得清楚明白。

4. 合同的制作比较正规，手续完整，不能更改。

Writing Requirements

When drafting a contract, one should:

First, use concrete and exact words in the contract; Second, be sure that the clauses will be complete; Third, keep the meaning of the contract clearly expressed and avoid being tampered.

（三）写作要求

1. 标题

需要写明合同的性质，如“借款合同”“财产租赁合同”。有的标题中还需写明标的物，如“××产品购销合同”。

2. 双方当事人的名称

书写签订合同双方当事人的名称，应当按营业执照上核准的名称写，要写全称，不能写简称，更不能写别人不了解的代称、代号。当事人的名称也不能简称甲方和乙方，应统一按照合同文本格式的规定书写。这种称谓不仅不便于行文表述，而且容易引起歧义。如，“工矿产品购销合同”中，称当事人为供方和需方；“财产租赁合同”中，称为出租方和承租方；“仓储保管合同”中，则称为存货方和保管方，等等。

3. 合同的正文一般包括以下几方面的内容：

（1）双方签订合同的依据和目的；（2）双方协商一致的内容。

4. 尾部

合同的尾部一般包括：双方当事人签章；签订合同的日期；如果需要双方主管部门证明或需要公证、鉴证的，要由有关单位写明意见，并加盖公章；合同的正、副本份数及合同的有效期限。

（文博等，2009）

Case Studies
二、案例分析

案例一

Sales Contract

This Agreement, entered into thisxx day of xx (m), xxxx (y) by and between The General Environmental Technos Co., Ltd., a corporation duly organized and existing under the laws of Japan and having its principal office of business at 1 - 3 - 5 Azuchi-cho, Chuo-ku, Osaka, Japan (hereinafter referred to as "Seller") and Buyer's name, a corporation duly organized and existing under the laws of Buyer's governing country and having its principal office of business at Buyer's address (hereinafter referred to as "Buyer"),

Witnesseth That:

WHEREAS, Seller develops and manufactures Products (defined below);

WHEREAS, Buyer desires to purchase Products from Seller, and Seller desires to sell Products to Buyer.

NOW, THEREFORE, it is agreed between the parties as follows:

Article 1. Purpose

1. Buyer agrees to purchase and Seller agrees to sell number of bottles and Lot number reference material for nutrients in seawater, RMNS, (contained in 100ml polypropylene bottle and individually wrapped and vacuum-sealed; hereinafter called "Products"), at the following contract price and upon the terms and conditions hereinafter set forth.

Contract Price: xx Japanese yen

2. Products shall be delivered in conjunction with the associated Identification of RMNS.

3. The trade term for the Contract Price is CIP (cost, insurance and

freight included) incompliance with the International Commercial Terms 2000 in Buyer's governing country, and the Contract Price may not be altered for whatsoever reason unless this Agreement is amended pursuant to Article 19. 2.

Article 2. Terms of Payment

Buyer shall pay the Contract Price to Seller in Japanese yen on or before the xx day of xx (m), xxxx (y) via wire transfer to the following bank account as designated by Seller.

Bank Name

SWIFT Code:

Savings Account No.

Account Holder: The General Environmental Technos Co. , Ltd.

Article 3. Delivery

Products shall be shipped to the destination designated by Buyer (hereinafter called the "Destination") via international courier service within 10 days following the date of full payment of the Contract Price (hereinafter called "Delivery Deadline") on the basis of CIP in compliance with the International Commercial Terms 2000, except as otherwise agreed upon in writing.

Article 4. Taxes

Both parties hereto shall pay any and all taxes imposed by law by their respective countries upon or on account of Products.

……

Article 18. Limitation of Seller's Liability

The amount of total aggregate liability to be born by Seller shall not exceed the total compensation received by Seller under this Agreement.

Seller shall not be liable to Buyer for any special or consequential damages, including but not limited to, lost profits, loss of use, and costs of replacement, caused by the Seller's negligence, breach of contract, or any other cause whatsoever.

Article 19. Entire Agreement and Amendment

1. This Agreement supersedes all prior negotiations, written communications, understandings and agreements relating to the subject hereof between the parties hereto.

2. This Agreement may not be amended or altered in any way other than written agreement between duly authorized representatives of respective parties hereto after the execution date hereof.

IN WITNESS WHEREOF, the parties hereto have caused this Agreement to be executed in two copies by their representatives or the persons duly authorized to execute this Agreement for each the party to retain one copy.

Buyers: (signature)

Sellers: (signature)

(文献来源：http: //www. kanso. co. jp/eng/production/pdf/sales_agreement. pdf, 检索日期：2015 年 9 月 8 日。)

Analysis

In terms of forms, the sales contract does not strictly accord with the format requirement of contract. However, it is quite clear about rights and liabilities of buyers and sellers, which suggests that the preparation of contract does not necessarily conform to one fixed format. Instead, it should demonstrate a certain degree of flexibility.

案例二

中外来件装配合同

甲方：__________电话: __________

法定代表人：__________职务: __________国籍: __________

乙方: __________电话：__________

法定代表人：__________职务: __________国籍: __________

兹经双方同意，甲方委托乙方在__________加工__________，其条款如下：

1. 来件装配的商品和数量：

（1）商品名称：

（2）数量共计: __________台。

2. 一切所需用的零件和原料由甲方提供，或由乙方在__________或__________购买，清单附于本合同内。

3. 每种型号的加工费如下：

（1）__________（大写：__________美元）；

（2）__________（大写：__________美元）；

（3）__________（大写：__________美元）；

4. 加工所需的主要零件、消耗品及原料由甲方运至__________，若有（某地）短少或破损，甲方应负责补充供应。

5. 甲方应于成品交运前一个月，开立信用证（或电汇全部加工费）用于由乙方在__________或__________购买零配件、消耗品及原料费用。

6. 乙方应在双方同意的时间内完成__________型标准__________的加工和交运，不得延迟，凡发生无法控制的和不可预见的情况例外。

7. 零件及原料的损耗率：加工时零件及原料损耗率为__________%，其损耗部分由甲方免费供应，如损耗率超过__________%，应由乙方补充加工所需之零件和原料。

8. 若甲方误运原料及零件，或错将原料及零件超运，乙方应将超运部分退回，其费用由甲方承担，若遇有短缺，应由甲方补充。

9. 甲方提供加工__________标准__________零件的原料，乙方应严格按规定的设计加工，不得变更。

10. 技术服务：

甲方同意乙方随时提出派遣技术人员到__________的要求，协助培训乙方的技术人员，并允许所派的技术人员留在乙方检验成品。为此，乙方同意支付每人月薪__________美元，其他一切费用（包括来回旅费）概由甲方负责。

11. 与本合同有关的一切进出口手续，应由乙方予以办理。

12. 加工后的标准＿＿＿＿＿乙方应运交给甲方随时指定的国外买主。

13. 其他条件：

（1）标准＿＿＿＿＿的商标由甲方提供，若出现法律纠纷，甲方应负完全责任；

（2）若必要时，乙方在＿＿＿＿＿或＿＿＿＿＿购买加工标准＿＿＿＿＿的零件及原料，其品质必须符合标准并事先需经甲方核准；

（3）为促进出口业务，乙方应储备标准＿＿＿＿＿样品，随时可寄往甲方所指定的国外买主，所需的零件和原料，由甲方所运来的零件及原料中报销。

14. 本合同一式两份，甲方与乙方在签字后各执一份。

甲方：＿＿＿＿＿　　乙方：＿＿＿＿＿

代表：＿＿＿＿＿　　代表：＿＿＿＿＿

＿＿＿＿＿年＿＿＿月＿＿＿日

（文献来源：许均秀主编：《商务合同签约范本（修订本）》，中国经济出版社 2008 年版，第 434 – 435 页。）

分析概要

从结构上看，中外来件装配合同基本符合合同的书写格式。项目、条款清晰，包括双方负责人较为详细的个人信息、商品名称和数量，双方权责规定清楚，是涉外商务合同中的一份典例。

Supplementary Readings

三、拓展阅读

请仔细阅读以下两则合同的内容，回答问题。

延长聘期合同

外国语学院（聘方）与__________先生（受聘方），根据共同的愿望，商定延长聘期________年，自__________年______月______日到__________年______月______日止。双方确认__________年______月______日原签订合同所列各项内容，在延长聘期的时间内继续有效。

聘方（签字）

受聘方（签字）

__________年______月______日于________

Reading Comprehension

Directions: Please give brief answers to the following questions.

1. 请简述以上合同的主要内容。
2. 思考该合同在措辞上是否有不妥，若有，请指出并改正。
3. 从内容上看，该合同是否全面？
4. 从形式上看，该合同是否完整，若不完整，请补充改正。

Technology Transfer Contract

This contract is signed in ______ on ______ 20 ______ .

Party A:

Party B:

Chapter 1

Content of the Contract

Party B shall be responsible for providing party A with the special technique of manufacturing, using and selling a series of plastic casters and related products in both written and unwritten form. The information concerning the kinds, specification and technical parameters of the contracted products manufactured by means of that technology is shown in detail in Attachment 1 of the contract.

Party B shall be responsible for arranging the training of the personnel of the Party A in the factory of Party B. Party B shall take effective measures to make the personnel of Party A have a good mastery of the technology, and experience in manufacturing the contracted products, as shown in detail in Attachment 2 of the contract.

Party B shall select and send qualified engineers to Party A's factory for technique advice, as shown in detail in Attachment 3 of the contract.

In selling the contracted products, Party A can use the trademarks of Party B or the registered trademarks of its own, as shown in detail in Chapter 8.

Chapter 2

Definition

The "contracted products" refer to the complete series of casters and related products listed in Attachment 1.

The "blue prints" refer to the copies of general drawings, production drawings, materials specifications and lists of machinery and parts, etc. which are used at present for manufacturing the contracted products or for improving design in future.

"Technical documentation" refers to the total technical know-how and its relevant design, circuit diagram and technical documents, etc., which are used at present for manufacturing the contracted products.

The "standard" refers to the one in the supplied documentation which is made and used by Party B for manufacturing the contracted products.

The technology transfer of contracted products shall be a one-time delivery.

The "term of the contract" refers to the duration of the cooperative joint venture company.

Chapter 3

Prices

According to the content stipulated in Chapter 1 of the contract, Party A shall pay Party B 500 thousand RMB as the contract costs, including the cost of drawings, documents, standard, specification, personnel training, and the transfer of the trade marks, etc.

The payment time of the contract costs shall be fixed through consultation between both Parties.

The contract is signed in ______, China by the authorized representatives of both parties on ______ of 20 ______ . The contract shall come into force beginning from the date of approval by the ______ City People's Government.

Party A: Party B:

Legal Representative: Legal Representative:

（文献来源：戚云方编：《合同与合同英语》，浙江大学出版社 2004 年版，第 362 页。）

Reading Comprehension

Directions: Please give brief answers to the following questions.

1. What is the main idea of this contract?
2. Can you generalize some basic features of the above contract?
3. What's the difference between the above contract and the usual contract?

7.4 Authorization
第四节 授权书

Basic Knowledge

一、基础知识

Introduction

Authorization, or letter of authorization or power of attorney, is an official form of approval for something which gives an official instruction or command. In business, it always refers to a document that states some contractual relationship.

When it is impossible for a person to be present to either take decisions regarding important legal or official matters or collect documents, it is possible to grant the authority to another person by means of an authorization letter. The letter has to be extremely precise and should leave absolutely no room for ambiguity. This is to prevent any instances of a misunderstanding.

（一）简介

授权书是授权人授权给受权人代表本级组织或本单位负责处理有关政务和业务，或者是授权机关或单位授权给受权机构或单位许可经营某项业务的证明性应用文书。

授权书适用于一级组织或一个单位内部以分配任务的形式进行的授权，如法人代表授权书等；也适用于某个机关或单位以许可经营的合约形式对外进行授权，如政府采购活动中的经营许可授权书等。

授权书的作用是权力的分配和责任的分担，有利于加强责任心，激励受权人创造性地完成某项政务或业务；就某个机关或单位以许可经营的合约形式对外进行授权而言，其作用是在责任分担前提下的业务专项管理和经营特约代理，有利于加强专业性，激励受权人独立自主地开拓发展经营活动。

（于成鲲等，2011）

Contents and Features

There are some dos and don'ts that you need to keep in mind, which are listed below.

1. The letter should be very clear about who is being entrusted with the authority to work on your behalf. Highlight their name if possible;
2. The reason for which the authority is being granted to the concerned

person should be stated clearly;

3. Always ensure that you mention the date on which the letter is issued to the holder;
4. Brevity is key. It is essential that important details are not missed out. A lengthy letter can often be tedious to read;
5. If applicable, include information about the period of validity of the letter;
6. Always check the letter for any spelling or grammatical errors.

（二）内容和特点

授权书其实就相当于授受双方约定权责关系的合同，它要对双方具有约束力，必须做到内容全面、准确。

1. 约束对象的规定：授权书必须详细列出受约束者，包括授权者、受权者、辅助人员。很多时候，授受双方可能都是以集体形式出现的。例如，董事会授权给一个工作小组，那么授权书就应列出这个集体的负责人姓名。辅助人员是指受权者可调用的人员或可向之进行咨询的人员。

2. 任务规定：对于受权者所接受的任务，授权书中应该有定义或限制。任务一般表现为执行具体的事情，组织内各任务的执行者所做的事情往往会有交叉的情况，授权书中应对这种可能出现的交叉情况进行限制，以避免重复工作。

3. 时间与成果规定：所有的授权工作都应有期限限制。时间的限制有刚性和弹性两种，刚性时间限制一般规定必须在某一时间点或某一期间内达到成果要求，弹性时间限制则只规定最后时间，具体在什么时间完成由受权者自由把握。成果则是管理者期望任务完成后的目标状态。成果可以表现为实物、金钱收益，也可以是精神性的，例如技术知识、道德水平、精神面貌的改变等。管理者不应将成果仅理解为可以得到的具体的东西。

4. 权力与责任关系规定：有了任务和目标成果，受权者的责任就有了依据。受权者没完成任务，将会受到什么样的惩罚就是责任的具体形式。管理者的责任是为受权者提供方便，管理者要尽可能确定自己所能提供的东西，以及确认如果没有提供这些东西，责任是否可以从受权者转移到管理者身上。双方的权力界限也需要明确，越过权力就会造成责任转移，这一项应在授权书中明确规定。

5. 资源调配的规定：授权书中应该列出受权者可以调动的各项资源，如资金、技术、信息、人员、物质资料等。这些资源应该尽可能地量化，使双方可以根据量化数字划定权力界限。资源调配不仅有数量问题，还有形式问题，受权者必须采用一定的文书形式调动资源，必须对资源的用途及使用结果做出说明。

授权书的特点主要包括：一是证明性，授权书是明确授权与受权、授责与受责合约关系的证明文书；二是授权性，权力的分配和许可的合约都以授权为前提；三是责任性，在授权之后有明确的责任分担的规定或约定；四是独立性，受权人在获得受权后有独立完成任务或经营特约代理的权力。

（卢小平，2011）

Writing Requirements

The letter of authorization is always including such parts as title, body, concluding remarks, signature and date. Please pay attention to the difference between this kind of document and others.

（三）写作要求

授权书的文本结构，依次由标题、正文、结语、署名、日期五部分组成。

1. 标题

标题或以授权者名称＋文种“授权书”为题，或以授权事项＋文种“授权书”为题。标题置于首页上方居中位置，字号稍大。

2. 正文

正文的内容主要是写明授权者与受权者的姓名或名称及其身份资料、授权事项、授权权限等。

3. 结语

结语是证明语或声明语。

4. 署名

署名是指授权者、受权者、相关者（证明者或投标者等）依次签名或盖章。署名置于结语下一行右侧。

5. 日期

日期是签署之日，置于署名下一行相应位置，年、月、日齐全，规范书写。

Case Studies

二、案例分析

案例一

Authorization

Annabeth Johnson

1204 A, Elm Street

732, Drake Bay

Tucson, AZ－85705

Jan 23, 2013

Sub: Authorization letter for Voyages Travel Agency.

To whomsoever it May Concern,

I, Annabeth Johnson authorize Voyages Travel Agency and their agents/appointed personnel to transport legal documents that are required to obtain a passport for myself.

I hereby grant permission to Voyages Travel Agency to act as my agent and give them the right to fulfill necessary obligations on my behalf in the process. I also grant them the authority to receive the passport.

I understand that Voyages Travel Agency will be in no way responsible for any delay caused in the course of processing and shipping.

Thanking you,

Sincerely,

A. Johnson（Signature）

Annabeth Johnson

（文献来源：http: //www. buzzle. com/articles/authorization-letter-sample. html, 检索日期：2016 年 3 月 2 日。）

Analysis

The authorization is written for obtaining passport. It includes title, date, body, concluding remarks, and signature. The body part has stated clearly the necessary information about authorization and responsibility of obtaining and receiving passport.

案例二

制造商出具的授权书

致: ________（制造商名称）

我们________（制造商名称）是按________（国家名称）法律成立的一家制造商，主要营业地点设在________（制造商地址）。

兹指派按________（合格来源国家名称）的法律正式成立的，主要营业地点设在________（贸易公司地址）的________（贸易公司名称）作为我方真正的合法性的代理人进行下列有效的活动：

代表我方在中华人民共和国办理贵方第×××号投标邀请要求提供

的由我方制造的货物的有关事宜，并对我方具有约束力。

作为制造商，我方保证以投标合作者来约束自己，并对该投标共同和分别承担招标文件中所规定的义务。

我方兹授予________（贸易公司名称）全权办理和履行我方为完成所有意图和目的而可能或可以做的一切必要的、必须的和适当的行为，并具有替换或撤销的全权。兹确认________（贸易公司名称）或其正式授权代表依此合法地办理一切事宜。

我方于××××年××月××日签署本文件，以此为证。

于××××年××月××日接受此件。

贸易公司名称

项目经理

授权代表签字，职位或职务，部门

制造商名称

中国销售部经理

授权代表签字，职位或职务，部门

（文献来源：梁寒主编：《国际商贸英文信函》，国防工业出版社 2009 年版，第 217 页。）

分析概要

这是一份制造商出具的授权书，从形式上看，基本合乎授权书的写作要求；内容也较为准确翔实，明确了制造商授权给贸易公司在目标国经营的法律依据；落款清晰明了。

Supplementary Readings

三、拓展阅读

请仔细阅读以下两则授权书的内容，回答问题。

商业授权书

××科技（中国）有限公司全球商业市场部兹授权××计算机技术有限公司代表××科技公司参与××××有限责任公司××建设工程。特此授权。

××科技公司将在技术、产品价格及售后服务等方面提供全力的支持。如有问题，请与××科技华南区办事处联系：×××××××××

××科技（中国）有限公司××办事处
2000年10月13日

Reading Comprehension

Directions: Please give brief answers to the following questions.

1. 请简述该商业授权书的主要内容及授权对象。
2. 从格式上看，该授权书是否符合要求？有无需要补充的地方？
3. 从内容上看，该授权书是否完整？
4. 简单总结本授权书的特点。

Letter of Authorization

Annabeth Johnson
1204 A, Elm Street
732, Drake Bay
Tucson, AZ－85705

Dear Dr. Payson,

Please release my medical records and other information related to the ACL tear treatment which I underwent under your medical supervision from Dec. 12, 2012 to Jan. 10, 2013, to Dr. Derreck Smith. The records will be used to assist further in my medical care. Please mail the records to:

Dr. Derreck Smith

Grace Hospital

1581, Lake Boulevard

Tucson, AZ - 85714

Thanking you,

Sincerely,

A. Johnson

(Signature)

(文献来源： http: //www. buzzle. com/articles/authorization-letter-sample. html, 检索日期：2016 年 2 月 12 日。)

Reading Comprehension

Directions: Please give brief answers to the following questions.

1. What is the main idea of this Authorization?
2. Can you generalize some basic features of the above Authorization?
3. Are there, if any, deficiencies in content of the above Authorization?
4. Try to improve the above Authorization.

7.5 Exercises
课后练习

- **True or False**

Directions: Read the following sentences and decide whether they are true or false.

1. Many letters of intent contain provisions that are binding.
2. A letter of intent is a contract and can be enforced.
3. An order confirmation is a commercial document and first official offer issued by a seller to a buyer.

4. A contract, essentially, is a promise or set of promises a court will enforce.
5. Legal contracts do include social obligations.
6. A contract, in the simplest definition, is a promise enforceable by law.
7. Contract is just a promise.
8. The original power of the attorney shall be attached with the bid; otherwise the bid might be automatically rejected.

• Gap-filling

Directions: Complete each sentence with appropriate words.

1. When writing a letter of intent, the ________, ________ and ________ should be appropriate to the situation intended for the letter you are about to write.
2. Acceptance of order confirmation by a seller forms a ________ between the buyer and seller, so no contract exists until the order confirmation is ________.
3. The ________ of contracts has to do with such questions as whether a contract exists, what the meaning of it is, whether a contract has been ________, and what compensation is due ________.
4. The ________ is properly signed by the persons or persons lawfully authorized by the bidder's legal person.

• Multiple Choices

Directions: In this part there are5incomplete sentences. For each sentence there are four choices marked A, B, C and D. Choose the ONE answer that best completes the sentence.

1. Letters of intent ________ written contracts, but are usually not binding on the parties in their entirety.

   A. are the same as　　　　B. resemble

C. unlike D. dislike

2. Order confirmation is used to control the ________ of products and services from external suppliers.

A. giving B. selling

C. purchasing D. rejecting

3. Contract is a promise, for breach of which the law gives remedy, or the performance of which the law in some way recognize as a ________.

A. duty B. habit

C. custom D. promise

4. The original power of the attorney shall be attached with ________, otherwise the bid might be automatically rejected.

A. the bid B. the agreement

C. the order D. the confirmation

5. The letter has to be extremely precise and should leave absolutely no roomfor ________.

A. ambiguity B. praise

C. criticism D. inquisition

• Translation

Directions: translate the following sentences into the target language.

English-Chinese translation

1. We are ready to perform the purchase agreement with seller with given terms and condition contained herein.
2. This is a non-binding letter of intent that contains provisions that are being discussed for a possible sale of the Business named above from the possible Seller named above to the possible Buyer named above.
3. We hereby confirm having sold to you the following goods on terms and conditions as set forth below.

4. Insurance: Buyers shall arrange insurance 110% of the invoice value and payable in Hong Kong in US currency.
5. In terms of any claim of shipment, notice of claim should be given in writing to sellers within 15 days after arrival of goods. If failing to do this, no claim will be entertained.
6. Party B shall bear responsibility for those taxes outside China arising from carrying out the contract.
7. In order to verify the reliability of the technical data provided by Party B and used for manufacturing the contracted products, a group for testing and inspection shall be composed by Party A and Party B, and the group shall be responsible for the practical operation of testing, inspecting and documenting results on the contracted products.

Chinese-English translation

1. 本意向书不应视为任何合同或具有法律约束力的协议，而应视作仅为磋商之目的而订立的有关本意向书项下可能达成之合同的条款概况。签署本意向书之目的是为了能够便于潜在买方就购买价格筹措资金。

2. 双方应对本意向书之内容保密，且除了本意向书项下双方及其雇员、律师、会计师和潜在买方之潜在贷款方之外，不得向任何其他第三方透露。

3. 买方须于 2001 年 5 月 1 日前将保兑的、不可撤销的、可转让的和可分割的即期信用证开到卖方。信用证议付有效期延至上述装运期后 15 天，在济南到期。

4. 若甲方误运原料及零件，或错将原料及零件超运，乙方应将超运部分退回，其费用由甲方承担，若遇有短缺，应由甲方补充。

5. 与本合同有关的一切进出口手续，应由乙方予以办理。

6. ××科技（中国）有限公司全球商业市场部兹授权××计算机技术有限公司代表××科技公司。

• Simulative Exercise

Foxconn is interested in establishing a joint venture with the Apple to produce 300000 mobile phones per year. On 1 January 2015, the two sides reached a preliminary agreement: Foxconn will offer a 6000 – square-meters land, 3 workshop buildings, 1 office building, as well as the power supply facilities, and other production and living facilities as investment. Apple Company will provide related technology, and equipment. This cooperation will last 20 years. The investment must be settled in US dollars for accounting. The investment proportion of China is 51% and the US is 49%. The staff of the joint venture will have 200 people. Before May 2015, the two sides should be ready for preparing relevant materials. In June, the Foxconn side should finish the project proposal and submit it to higher authorities. After approved by authorities, they should immediately notify Apple Company. Please formulate the letter of intent, both in English and Chinese.

8 Notes for Classical Chinese Writings
第八章 中文信函中常用文言词汇注释

中华人民共和国成立以后，国务院发布了关于推广汉语普通话和汉语规范化的指示，我们应该在一切领域，为祖国语言的健康和发展做出贡献。

在语言的实际应用中，一方面，对于文言文我们的原则是不用不写；另一方面，目前在中外合营企业和广泛的国际经济贸易交往中，许多地区和国家都在使用汉文函件，如香港地区、澳门地区、台湾地区，以及新加坡、日本等。世界其他各地为数众多的华侨也在使用汉文信函与我们进行直接的、频繁的交往，但他们使用的汉文函件有别于中国内地经过改革发展后的中文，其中包括较多的文言词汇。为了方便阅读和写作，我们将常用的文言词汇注释如下。

8.1 Form of Address
第一节 称呼部分

台鉴——“台”：旧时对别人的敬称。“鉴”：审阅的意思。“台鉴”即“您审阅”。

例：×××先生台鉴……

台览——“览”：“看”“阅”的意思。“台览”即“您阅”。

例：经理先生台览……

惠鉴——“惠”：施惠。“惠鉴”是有求于人时的敬称，即“劳驾您审阅”。

例：×××先生惠鉴……

雅鉴——“雅”：谓对方高雅，而且其中含有“雅正”的意思。“雅鉴”即“请您审阅并指教”。

例：×××先生雅鉴……

钧鉴——对尊长、上级的敬辞。

例：×××先生钧鉴……

8.2 Body Part

第二节 正文部分

贵——“尊贵”，对别人的敬称。例：贵公司来函收悉。

敝——对自己的谦称。例：关于洽谈一事，敝公司将派人前往。

悉——“知道”“了解”的意思。例：6月5日来函已悉。

谨悉——谨：表示尊敬。谨悉：“恭敬地了解到”。例如，来函谨悉。

兹——“现在”“此”。例：兹有我公司×××先生前往洽谈。

兹启者——启：“说”“陈述”。兹启者：“现在说的、陈述的”。例如，兹启者，裘皮加工合约事实上已经撤销。

顷接——顷：“刚才”。顷接：“刚才接到”。例如，顷接来函询问租船一事……

鉴于——“由于考虑到”的意思。例如，鉴于我公司目前货源紧缺……

拟于——“打算在”的意思。例如，我们公司拟于下月中旬派代表团前往贵国。

就绪——即“已经安排好”。例如，春交会筹备工作业已就绪。

业经——“已经、经过”的意思。例如，贵方提出的要求，业经我方研究通过。

逞（径）与——即“直接与”。例如，关于信用证一事，请逞与×××先生联系。

系——即“是”。例如，经技术鉴定，纯系质量问题。

显系——“显然是”。例如，这批货物的破损，显系装运责任。

度即——度：“继续”。即：“立即”。例如，如贵公司尚有异议，请度即函告。

销罄——罄：“空”，引申为“尽”“完”，这里是“售完”的意思。例如，我存货已销罄。

讫——“终了”“完毕”之意。例如，贵公司寄来清单验讫……

一体——即“一律”。例如，上述商品一体按合同价格交售。

竭诚——“竭尽全力、真心实意”。例如，感谢贵公司竭诚合作。

藉——即“凭借”。例如，藉此表达我们对贵公司的真诚谢意。

歉难——即“抱歉、难以”。例如，此次事故责任不在我方，歉难承担经济损失。

俾——“使”的意思。例如，请于××月××日前来电确认，俾客制约。

暨——“及”的意思。例如，××月××日来函暨附订单一份，均已收悉。

8.3 Concluding Part

第三节 结尾部分

函达——“写信告知”。例如，特此函达。

见复——“得到答复”。例如，希望速予办理见复。

查照——“查看”。例如，希查照办理为荷。

为荷——荷，即“承受别人的恩惠”。为荷，可以理解为“感谢你们的帮助”。例如，请您于5月前将贵公司函告我方为荷。

复希——“还希望”。例如，复希将查照结果告知。

台安——“您安好”。例如，敬祝台安。

台祺——“您吉祥、福气”。例如，顺颂台祺。

台绥——“您平安”。例如，即颂台绥。

近祉——祉：“福”的意思。近祉，即“近来幸福”。例如，此问近祉。

时祉——“现在幸福”。例如，祝时祉。

谨泐（lè）——泐：“写”的意思。谨泐，即“恭敬地书写”。例如，×××公司王达谨泐。

谨复——“恭敬地答复”。例如，中华商会××谨复。

谨启——启：“陈述”。谨启：“恭敬地陈述”。例如，纺织品公司×××谨启。

亲启——启：“打开、启封”。亲启：“亲自阅读”。例如，×××亲启。

8.4 Others
第四节　其他

莅临——“到来”。例如，敬请莅临。

下榻——榻：“狭长而较矮的床”，或泛指床。下榻：“留宿、休息”。例如，在×××饭店下榻。

令闻——“旧时美好名声”。例如，贵公司旧有令闻。

令尊——称对方父亲的敬辞。

令堂——称对方母亲的敬辞。

令郎——称对方儿子的敬辞。

令爱——称对方女儿的敬辞。

Recommendations

推荐书目

Appadorai, A. （1982）. *Select Documents on India's Foreign Policy and Relations, 1947 – 1972*（*Vol. 2*）. Oxford University Press.

Baker, J. A. （1995）. *The Politics of Diplomacy: Revolution, War, and Peace, 1989 – 1992*. Putnam Adult.

Bayne, N., & Woolcock, S. （Eds.）. （2011）. *The New Economic Diplomacy: Decision-making and Negotiation in International Economic Relations*. Ashgate Publishing, Ltd.

Berridge, Geoff R., and Lorna Lloyd. （2012）. *The Palgrave Macmillan Dictionary of Diplomacy*. Palgrave Macmillan.

Gambone, M. D. （2002）. *Documents of American Diplomacy: From the American Revolution to the Present*. Greenwood Publishing Group.

Hill, C., & Smith, K. E. （2000）. *European Foreign Policy: Key Documents*. Psychology Press.

Jönsson, C., and Martin Hall. （2005）. *Essence of Diplomacy*. Houndmills: Palgrave Macmillan.

Rana, K. S. （2011）. *21st-Century Diplomacy: A Practitioner's Guide*. Bloomsbury Publishing USA.

Roeder, L. W., and Albert Simard. （2013）. *Diplomacy and Negotiation for Humanitarian NGOs*. Springer.

柏莹主编：《应用文写作教程》，哈尔滨工业大学出版社 2011 年版。

蔡践：《新编公务员实用写作》，中国国际广播出版社 2005 年版。

陈纪宁编：《21 世纪应用文写作大全》，内蒙古大学出版社 2004 年版。

陈永国、郑淑媛、陈智钢：《新编英语应用文写作》，江西高校出版社 2009 年版。

程道德等编：《中华民国外交史资料选编 1919－1931》，北京大学出版社 1988 年版。

戴萍：《商务应用文写作教程》，中国对外经济贸易出版社 2007 年版。

戴盛才主编：《中文应用写作教程》，复旦大学出版社 2011 年版。

冬梅：《中美关系资料选编（1971. 7－1981. 7）》附：中美关系大事记，时事出版社 1982 年版。

段芹、丁金国编著：《涉外应用文写作全书》，山东人民出版社 1994 年版。

范浩鸣、阳晴、黄宏丰、韦韩克等：《最新公务文书写作全编》，气象出版社 2008 年版。

方建文、李啸尘主编：《国际事务领导全书（第 2 卷）》，国际文化出版公司 2002 年版。

方贤华：《实用政务大词典》，湖北辞书出版社 1993 年版。

关彤主编：《交际写作》，北京师范大学出版社 1999 年版。

郭英立主编：《经济应用文写作》，清华大学出版社 2012 年版。

黄德禄、黄安年选译：《世界史资料丛刊——1917－1939 年的美国》，商务印书馆 1990 年版。

黄金祺编：《英汉对照外交文献文书教程》（上册），世界知识出版社 2004 年版。

黄金祺编：《英汉对照外交文献文书教程》（下册），世界知识出版社 2004 年版。

江永海编：《新世纪办公室管理规范全书》，吉林大学出版社 2001 年版。

金波编：《职业经理商务写作能力训练》，高等教育出版社 2004 年版。

黎孟德:《实用应用文大全:规范、实用、权威的应用文范文》,成都时代出版社 2004 年版。

李德芳等主编:《应用文写作》,北京师范大学出版社 1999 年版。

李家发:《外交外事知识及国际交往礼仪》,广西师范大学出版社 2008 年版。

李薇编:《会展文案》,广东高等教育出版社 2014 年版。

李啸尘编:《办公室工作标准运作典范全书·公文写作秘书卷》,中国言实出版社 2001 年版。

廉正保、王景堂、黄韬鹏:《解密外交文献——中华人民共和国建交档案》(1949 - 1955),中国画报出版社 2006 年版。

梁寒编:《国际商贸英文信函》,国防工业出版社 2009 年版。

廖雄军等编:《实用涉外文书写作》,广西人民出版社 1995 年版。

刘俊昌主编:《现代经济贸易应用文写作》,安徽人民出版社 2001 年版。

刘战英:《新时期办公室主任手册》,新华出版社 2006 年版。

刘志伟编:《国际商务函电》,对外经济贸易大学出版社 2011 年版。

冒志祥编著:《宋朝的对外交往格局——论宋朝外交外事文书形态》,广陵书社 2012 年版。

潘新明编著:《外事实用文书大全》,辽宁人民出版社 1994 年版。

钱其琛主编:《世界外交大辞典》,世界知识出版社 2005 年版。

任焕琴编:《公共关系实用教程》,北京大学出版社 2012 年版。

[美] 塞林格、[法] 洛朗著,廖先旺等译:《海湾战争:秘密档案》,世界知识出版社 1991 年版。

史玉峤:《现代文秘写作》,青岛出版社 2004 年版。

粟斌编:《新编应用写作简明教程》,科学出版社 2012 年版。

苏鹏编:《国际贸易书信》,新联书社 1986 年版。

王保华、齐明敏、张宏编著:《阿拉伯政治外交与中阿关系》(下),外语教学与研究出版社 2002 年版。

吴瑞玲主编:《新编经济应用写作》,知识产权出版社 2011 年版。

向常华、叶昌德编:《现代常用文体写作全书:实用涉外文书写作大全》，哈尔滨地图出版社 2005 年版。

谢世洋编：《应用文写作理论与实践》，清华大学出版社 2014 年版。

萧枫编：《办公室文书写作大全》，中国人事出版社 2001 年版。

肖莉编：《酒宴交际实用全书》，中国人口出版社 2007 年版。

辛业江著：《常用公文写作》，三环出版社 1990 年版。

于云、王力等编：《企业外交实用文体写作》，中国经济出版社 1990 年版。

曾富蓉、黄大勇：《涉外文书规范写作》，重庆出版社 2002 年版。

张浩编：《最新行政公文写作技巧、格式、模板与实用范例全书》，海潮出版社 2014 年版。

张浩清：《外贸实务疑难解惑 220 例》，中国海关出版社 2012 年版。

张建国、贾晓航、刘英侠编著：《中国外事管理实务》，知识产权出版社 2005 年版。

张文贤编：《国际惯例词典》，复旦大学出版社 2000 年版。

郑仰成编：《电力英语应用文写作》，中国水利水电出版社 2003 年版。

《中国领事工作》编写组编：《中国领事工作》（下册），世界知识出版社 2014 年版。

周邦友编著：《英语应用文大典》，中国科学技术大学出版社 1997 年版。

周鲠生：《国际法》（下），武汉大学出版社 2009 年版。

周国宝、张慎霞编著：《外事管理实务》，华南理工大学出版社 2005 年版。

祝雪虎：《经济文书写作技巧、模板与范例》，广东经济出版社 2008 年版。

新华网：http: //news. xinhuanet. com。

中国礼仪网：http: //www. welcome. org. cn。

中华人民共和国外交部网站：http: //www. fmprc. gov。

中华人民共和国中央人民政府网站：http: //www. gov. cn/ztzl/zmbh/content_624348. htm。